The Diabetes Game

A Teenager's Guide to Living Well with Diabetes

by Nora Coon

Published by
Rewarding Health, Inc.
5440 SW Westgate Drive #175
Portland, OR 97221-2420
503.297.3334 ext. 13
www.rewardinghealth.net

ISBN: 0-9778355-0-2

Printed in the United States of America.
Distributed to the book trade by Rewarding Health, Inc.

Publisher's Cataloging-in-Publication Data

The diabetes game: a teenager's guide to living well with diabetes/Nora
Coon
        p. cm
Summary: A teenager offers guidance on living with diabetes, on topics
such as diet, school, social life, and family issues.

In memory of Dr. Eugene L. Coodley,
who never got to give his diagnosis.

This book is for everyone who's ever been asked,
"Doesn't that hurt?"
and for those
who have to think a moment before answering.

Also by Nora Coon

It's Your Rite: Girls' Coming-of-Age Stories
Teen Dream Jobs

For more information about Nora's work, check out www.noracoon.smartwriters.com or www.diabetesgame.blogspot.com.

Acknowledgements

This book owes its existence to a great many people, who I'm afraid I must list with zero explanation as to my reasons: Dr. David Snyder, Dr. Maya Hunter, Dr. Marcia Coodley, Dr. Mike Fulop, Bart MacGillivray, Karen, Sara, Darcy, and Maria of Emanuel Hospital, the entire faculty and staff of the Catlin Gabel Upper School, everyone at the Gales Creek Camp, and Brynna Hurwitz and the Children's Diabetes Network.

Finally, this book came about because of my long-suffering parents, Cheryl and Jim Coon, who are not only to blame for my existence but also for helping me past all the rough spots, both with this book and with my life in general. Sorry guys, it's the truth.

Table of Contents

Foreword

Frederick Nietzsche, a famous Prussian philosopher, wrote this often quoted line: *"What does not destroy me makes me stronger."* While this notion is mainly true, Frederick either missed or merely passed over the more frequently experienced form of this sentiment: *"What does not destroy me pisses me off a lot."* Also, the "über philosopher" did not have Type 1 diabetes. Nor was he an adolescent, ever. So, the sad truth is Nietzsche wrote nothing about surviving diabetes with your teenage soul intact. If you find yourself doing the diabetes two-step (Test–Shot!–Test) and are a teen with diabetes (or perhaps a best friend or parent of a teen with diabetes) Nora Coon has written a very helpful guide for you.

You may recognize that Nora's voice is not all sweetness and cheeriness about diabetes. She is honest about what she feels and thinks. Chapter topics - leaving the hospital, dances, alcohol, and travel plans - make it clear Nora doesn't judge and she is above all a realist. She lives in the same world you live in. Also, Nora pulls no punches about coping. Nora covers areas diabetes manuals and health care providers miss or dare not touch.

Yet, as a psychologist, I find that Nora's most important messages are embedded within her approach to surviving diabetes. In the introduction Nora tipped her hand and it grabbed my attention from a first reading. She writes:

> *"This book is about learning to make diabetes a normal part of your normal life, and maybe – possibly – turning diabetes into an advantage. Don't laugh. It's possible."*

Nora tells you her story about coping with diabetes without being preachy. She doesn't imply understanding of everybody's problems and experiences. She doesn't say to do everything she says, or even what your doctor says, but she advocates that you **be active in taking care of yourself**. Nora's words find the heart and muscle of day-to-day diabetes – learning to self-manage as much as you can and should, and trusting and depending on those whose help you require.

Nora provides another two vital messages early in her survival guide. The first is that your emotions can be useful and valuable. Nora's twist on this is — don't waste time blaming others; pack your emotions with you, but don't think they get you all that you need or want as a person. The second message will take you quite a while to get your head around: "Make diabetes work for you."

Though diabetes and the chores and changes it entails is neither simple nor easy, it is doable, and **it can be made to fit in your life**. Nora faces the pain and sorrow of diabetes, the day-to-day reality of it, and shows how you can move diabetes to the "minimized screen" state, not the whole computer screen. Above all, Nora's survival guide is a book of coping, resilience and heart. It reminds me of a very old quote from the Talmud: "Live well. It is the greatest revenge." Nora's attitude might change that to: *"Live well with diabetes. It's a great revenge."*

-- Dr. Mike Fulop

December 27, 2005

Chapter 1 - Introduction

June 3, 2000. Saturday. My friend Nicole slept over. She ran around, rode our horse, went swimming, and did all the things a normal fifth-grade girl would do, while I dragged myself around after her and, at one point, took a nap. She couldn't understand why I didn't want to play.

June 4, 2000. Sunday. Nicole went home, disappointed because we'd planned to stay up all night watching movies and I'd fallen asleep at 8:30 pm and hadn't gotten up until 11 am.

June 5, 2000. Monday. I trudged through school, trying to stay awake and cut down the number of times I got up to get a drink and go to the bathroom. After school, my mom picked me up and told me that we were going to see the doctor because I'd been so tired. Three hours and about a pint of blood later, I was in a hospital bedroom, crying and clutching my new stuffed animals.

If someone gave you this book and you chose to read it, chances are you had a similar experience. Maybe you were only two years old when you were diagnosed and you don't remember it at all. Maybe you were seven and it's a faded memory. Maybe you were my age and it's still fresh enough to be slightly raw. Or maybe (and if so, you have my heartfelt sympathy) you've just been diagnosed. No matter what your circumstances, it sucks.

But this book isn't about pity parties (which, by the way, can be extremely fun and are highly recommended every once in a while. See Chapter 7 on diabetes burnout). This book is about learning to make diabetes a normal part of your normal life, and maybe – possibly – turning diabetes into an advantage. Don't laugh. It's possible.

I am not a big believer in the whole "every-cloud-has-a-silver-lining" theory. I've seen plenty of bad things happen with zero benefit. Diabetes, though, does come with certain benefits, and that's why I wrote this book – to help you figure out how to use them.

WHO I AM

I'm seventeen. In June of 2000, I was diagnosed with juvenile diabetes. All I knew about diabetes at the time was what I'd learned from the Baby-Sitters Club book. One of the babysitters, Stacey, ends up in the hospital after eating some chocolate.

It took me a good amount of hating diabetes and rebelling against it to realize that I was being counterproductive. I could have been using that energy in a much better way. So I wrote this book to help you avoid my mistakes. Once you know how to deal with it, diabetes can get filed under "another irritating hurdle in your life." Don't waste your time snapping at your endocrinologist and being irresponsible just to irritate your parents – please, put it to better use. Make diabetes work for you.

HOW TO USE THIS BOOK

Unless you've only just been diagnosed with diabetes and are still in the hospital, you really don't need to read straight through the entire book. I understand that you have homework to do, friends to see, a life to have...and there's no benefit gained by strapping yourself to a chair and reading this for however long it takes you to finish it.

The Diabetes Game is designed so that you can read what you need, when you want, and still get all the benefits. Each chapter is self-contained; read Chapter 6 when school and diabetes collide or Chapter 7 when you start to burn out on diabetes. Keep this book around for when you're a couple years into diabetes and – like me – need an occasional reminder as to what you're supposed to be doing.

If you've just been diagnosed with diabetes, I recommend that you work your way straight through the first six chapters. I put them in that order because that's how you usually will run into the assorted issues and problems, and I promise that it will make better sense that way.

Finally, remember that what I'm telling you isn't your doctor's advice. All I can do is share with you, from the point of view of another teenager, a sense of how I've handled nearly 6 years of diabetes and what I've learned from it. After that, you're on your own and should talk to your doctor about any questions you have.

Either way, I'd like to hear from you. Contact me through the Diabetes Game website at www.diabetesgame.blogspot.com. So let's go.

Chapter 2 – Hospital to Home

The main difference between the hospital and your home (aside from significantly better food) is that once you arrive home, you won't have a team of doctors and nurses checking on you every three seconds. Suddenly you've lost the support network ready to rush in with an assortment of juices 24/7 if you go low. Or the trained endocrinologist who's always available to fine-tune your insulin doses.

When you get home, you and your parents are responsible for keeping you healthy – or alive, anyway. Moving from the hospital to home is a big jump, especially when your life has just been permanently changed.

In the hospital, if something goes wrong, they have thousands of dollars' worth of medical equipment to make sure that you're okay until they can fix whatever the problem was. If you have an emergency, all that stands between you and perfect health is being wheeled into the ICU. A team of professionals focuses solely on you.

At home, though, things are different. The rest of the world isn't so interested in your problems. When something goes wrong with diabetes, you and your family have to fix it with your own knowledge of diabetes. To reach your doctor, you usually have to go through levels of hospital bureaucracy or an ambulance ride (which is not nearly as exciting as the rest of the world seems to think).

It's the little things that count. The difference between diabetes in the hospital and diabetes at home is like the difference between diving into a pool knowing exactly how deep it is and diving blindfolded, without knowing whether the pool even has water in it. Sometimes you might get lucky, but you also might bash your head open.

YOUR TRANSITION TIME

It takes a while to get used to diabetes (understatement!). Everyone else will try to be very understanding – even *too* understanding – for a few days, or a week. Your parents will probably feel so guilty that they'll work hard to understand for maybe a month. But at a certain point, people will expect you to move on with your life – to 'get over it'.

To be frank...that's never going to happen. You will adjust, eventually, but you'll never get over it. Getting diabetes changes your life, and even if you stay healthy, your body and the way you look

STAYING ON TRACK

At this point, it's all about remembering what they taught you in the hospital: What to do when you're low, what to do when you're high, how to manage your diet and injections – all while keeping up some semblance of normality. This is the time when you should remember to check your blood sugar, take your injections, and eat within your meal plans.

Hey, be proud of yourself – you've gotten this far. Some people are back in the hospital within a week because they simply can't handle everything that's happened to them. It's okay if you find yourself slamming doors with just a little more force than necessary – that's a totally normal and acceptable response. If your parents fault you for it, suggest that they take part in the diabetes simulation (Chapter 9.)

at the world will always be a little different. So don't worry about how long it takes you to adjust. That said, you can only avoid the outside world for so long. While your parents are still being super-lenient (or, barring that, super-sympathetic), try to ease your way back into your usual routine. This is, of course, easier if your usual routine involves healthy food and plenty of exercise. If it consists of salt, sugar, homework, and TV like mine did, you may have a bit more work ahead. I think the key is to go in stages. Don't leave the hospital and expect to be a fully functioning human being. That transformation occurs while you're at home, gradually.

WHO DOES WHAT

When you first get home from the hospital, your parents may be eager to do everything for you. They'll go to a lot of trouble to make you as

---

TOP MOVIES <u>NOT</u> TO WATCH RIGHT AFTER GETTING DIABETES

1. *Charlie and the Chocolate Factory*. Why torture yourself? Give it a year until you've got an insulin pump and can eat whatever you want.
2. *Chocolat*. See above re: torture.
3. *Panic Room*. You thought your low blood sugars were bad? Take my word for – Jodie Foster's daughter's are worse. And *she's* trapped without medical supplies. Whatever you do, don't let your parents see it. Or do, if you're looking for a bit of entertainment, and see how they react the next time you go low and don't have a fast sugar.
4. *Steel Magnolias*. The diabetic dies. Not exactly cheerful, keep-your-spirits-up fare. A World War II buddy film like *The Dirty Dozen* might be a little happier.

---

comfortable as they can, run up huge bills at the video store, and generally treat you like an invalid. This way of life is very enjoyable for a few days – but then your parents (and the rest of the world) begin to expect that you will get used to it, which is close to getting over it – they want you to return to your 'normal' life.

The ideal time to divide the responsibilities with your parents is when they still feel terrible and want to do whatever they can to make your life easier. If this sounds too manipulative for you, ignore my advice and see how you feel in a few years.

YOUR RESPONSIBILITIES
- test your blood sugar
- take shots
- calculate carbohydrate values
- learn more about diabetes

YOUR PARENTS' RESPONSIBILITIES
- pay for medical care
- learn more about diabetes
- remind you to do diabetes tasks
- take care of you in emergencies

NEGOTIABLE
- give injections

- record blood sugar values
- wake up in the middle of the night after lows to test

As you get older, you'll have to take on more of the responsibilities that used to belong to your parents, so that by the time you move out, you'll be fully capable of taking care of yourself. I found that the best way to divide jobs when it comes to diabetes is to sit down at the table with your parents (send your siblings elsewhere – sometimes they'll help you out, but sometimes they'll hurt your case) and have a calm, rational discussion.

Prepare your arguments beforehand about what you each should have to do, and be ready to give a timetable for when you'll start to take on more responsibilities. The timetable will be especially important if you plan to ask your parents to give you injections; you can't keep up that arrangement forever.

REGAINING LOST WEIGHT

Unless someone caught on early to the fact that you'd gotten diabetes, you probably lost a lot of weight in the process of getting diabetes. You lose the weight because your body can't get any energy from sugar (no insulin to let sugar into the cells), so it starts to break down fat and protein instead. You lose a lot of muscle too.

People may not notice it at the time, but if you go back and compare what you looked like six months ago to what you look like now, you'll see a frightening difference. I lost fifteen pounds in approximately three weeks, and looked like something out of a horror movie.

Once you go on insulin, you'll start to gain the weight back, fast. Some anorexic people with diabetes don't take their insulin because insulin usually helps you gain weight. This is, of course, an incredibly dangerous way to lose weight, since you're depriving yourself of vital medication and nutrients in food.

The best thing to do is accept the fact that you really do need to gain back the fifteen or twenty pounds you lost. Then, focus on keeping your eating healthy. You know, eat your fruits and vegetables, make sure you get plenty of protein, don't eat too much, etc. etc. Eating can become a problem for a lot of us with diabetes.

FINALLY...take home messages

The transition from hospital life back to your 'normal' life is not easy, especially since you can never truly return to your "old life". But you will be able to survive outside the hospital. Enjoying life again...well, that comes later. For now, focus on making it to the next day. I'm not sure how long it took me to readjust. I've completely erased most of that first summer from my memory. But I know that eventually I did adjust – and my life got better.

Chapter 3 – Needles

For many people, needles are the worst part of diabetes. At least, that's true at first. But – speaking as someone who used to scream whenever my mom brought me within fifty feet of a doctor's office for a shot – insulin shots are the mildest shots that you will ever take. Even better, it's not a nurse who has to do another forty teenagers after you; it's you or your parents. Three months into diabetes and I guarantee you'll be used to the shots – just in time to start going crazy about your restrictive diet. But until then, here's a little help with the freakiest part of diabetes.

Insulin injections are subcutaneous, meaning that you inject the insulin just below and into your skin. Subcutaneous injections are the *least* painful kind of injection. When you get a flu shot, it's intramuscular – it goes into your muscle – which is why it's so painful and why you get so sore. When you're in the hospital and they have to put you on a continuous flow of a fluid, you get an IV needle – intravenous. The needle goes into your vein.

YOUR PARENTS

Many people, especially when they first get diabetes, just can't handle sticking a needle into their own bodies. That's normal, but it means that you'll have to take your shots from your parents. For more on handling parents and diabetes, see Chapter 8.

First, figure out which of your parents will give you your shots. In my case, it was my mom, but you may work better with your dad or even an older brother or sister (this isn't really advisable, though – letting someone with whom you routinely fight stick something sharp in you? Bad idea.).

Once you know who gives the shots, decide where on your body the shots go. Your doctor may have specific areas that he or she wants you to inject at certain times of day, but the basic three are arm, thigh, and stomach.

BENEFITS OF GIVING YOURSELF SHOTS

If you give yourself your injections, you're able to control how fast the needle goes in and how fast you actually take the insulin. You also don't have to drag a parent with you everywhere you plan to eat – this is very convenient if you happen to go to a party or sleep over at someone's house. It's also viewed as part of the progression towards independence and college.

Some people start out giving themselves their own shots; it takes a little longer for others. It was six weeks before I could actually face the thought of giving myself shots, but after that, I never let my parents do it again. Some people (the rip-Band-Aids-off group) like to do everything very, very quickly; others, like me, can't bear that sort of thing and take needles slowly. It's your choice – though you'll have a lot more control over it if you're the one giving the shot.

ARM INJECTIONS

Your arm is probably the most convenient place for a shot, but you'll absorb the insulin faster. Hold your arm straight out, with the thumb upward, and feel the fat on the bottom of your upper arm. That's where you give the shot. If you have very thin arms – which you may, since getting diabetes can make you lose a lot of weight – you may be better off using a different area.

To give yourself a shot in your arm, sit down somewhere flat. Prop your knee up on your seat and use it to spread out the loose area of your arm, as shown in the diagram. Alternatively, you can use the back of a chair. Just make sure you're in a position you could hold for a long time – it's not a good idea to be all twisted up and jumping around while you're trying to give yourself a shot.

Insert the needle at a ninety-degree angle (perpendicular to your arm). Very carefully, lift your arm so that the fat is no longer pinched up, and push down on the plunger until all the insulin has gone into your arm. It's important that your arm isn't pinched when the insulin enters it, because otherwise it can leak out. Once all the insulin is in your arm, wait a second and then remove the needle. It's okay if a little blood appears, but it shouldn't bleed a lot.

See the diagram for an illustration of where best to give/take a shot in your arm

THIGH INJECTIONS

Shots in your thigh are usually the least painful because that's where you have the most fat. Pinch up the area on the outside of your thigh. The needle should be inserted perpendicular to your leg. Gently release the thigh fat so that your leg is its normal shape, and push down on the syringe plunger. Then remove the syringe.

See the diagram for an illustration of where best to give/take a shot in your thigh.

STOMACH INJECTIONS

You can also take a shot in your stomach. If you have enough fat to be able to do this, you can tell. If your stomach is muscled or if you have a completely flat stomach, you should probably skip injecting into your stomach and just go with your thigh. Stomach injections are particularly hard for other people to give to you, so you're better off doing it on your own or not at all.

Pinch up the fat on your stomach and insert the needle, then *very carefully* let go of the fat. If you do it carelessly, the needle will fall out and you'll have to do it all over again. Which, when you're still afraid of needles, is kind of a pain (sorry, bad pun). Inject the insulin and remove the needle. Again, you really shouldn't bleed. A little bit is acceptable – like if you scratch yourself badly – but if it's actually running, something's probably wrong.

See the diagram on the next page for an illustration of where best to give/take a shot in your stomach.

TESTING, TESTING, 1-2-3-4

Okay, I have to be honest. Testing your blood sugars hurts a lot more than giving yourself shots. This is because you have tons of nerves in your fingers (one reason you use them to feel things),

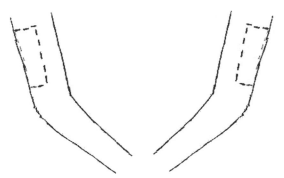

Left and right arms - give shot in outside of arm.

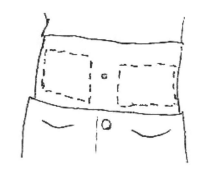

Stomach - give shot on either side.

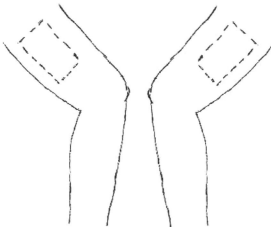

Left and right legs - give shot in outside of thigh.

whereas you have no nerves in your fat. The testing needles are about the same width as syringes, although syringe needles are hollow and testing needles ('lancets') are usually shorter.

Unfortunately, you usually test blood sugars more often than you give yourself shots, and you will probably develop scars in the form of lots of little dark pinprick marks up and down the sides of your fingertips, unless you're very careful and never use the same finger twice to test. Of course, this is unlikely, seeing as how you have only ten fingers and will need to test your blood sugar more than ten times in your life.

That said, testing is another one of those things that gets to be very natural. After a couple of years of diabetes, you won't really recall what it was like not to test before every meal. And despite the fact that it does hurt, because you test so often you start to develop a certain disconnect between your brain and your fingertips – you're aware, somewhere in your brain, that what you just did was painful, but you're so used to it that the pain doesn't really cause a reaction, aside from the obligatory "Ow."

Ideally, you should wash your hands before you test, and use a Kleenex or something to blot your finger. I have to say, though, that once you get past the "I'm-a-good-diabetic-and-will-do-everything-perfectly" phase and into the "I'm-so-sick-of-all-this phase", you will forget about this. No sink within several inches? You'll find that you just wipe your fingers clean on your shirt before testing. Even if there's a box of Kleenex sitting right next to you when you test, the knee-jerk reaction is to put your finger in your mouth – despite everything you've heard about how incredibly dirty the inside of your mouth is. It's natural – don't worry too much about it at all. No one stays perfect forever.

The important thing is to test within five minutes before you eat. Even if you're having, say, eggs, bacon, and hash browns, you should test *before* eating anything, not after eating the eggs and bacon but before the hash browns. Although the eggs and bacon won't affect your blood sugar, the idea is to get in the habit of always testing before you eat. This is the best way to train yourself.

THE BASICS

Okay, basic mechanics of testing. Squeeze blood up into the top segment of your finger (this isn't necessary, but it can help). When you're starting out and are likely to jerk your finger away from the needle, you should probably put your

28

finger against a hard surface (such as a table) to keep it steady. Line up the spring-loaded little testing needle with the correct area of your finger – most people use the inside and outside of the top half-centimeter of each finger. You get the maximum amount of blood, the least pain, and the least disruption of your normal activity (i.e. you can still use your finger). Wipe the blood on your testing strip, and clean the remaining blood off your finger.

Depending on your meter, you'll have the results in 5-45 seconds. If you get an error message, figure out what you did wrong and try again. There's really no point to bandaging your finger; it'll stop bleeding within seconds, and a Band-Aid will only interfere with its use.

TESTING IN EXTREME CONDITIONS

As you might have noticed, for most medical equipment there is an optimal temperature at which it needs to be stored, and this is true for insulin and test strips as well. Your meter might not work if it gets too cold or hot. Use common sense – don't leave your meter, tests strips, or insulin sitting in the sun, in your car on a hot day, or in the freezer (not that you would put your meter in the freezer).

If you're looking for specific strategies for testing in challenging conditions, such as skiing, hiking in the desert, and flying, read Chapter 10 on travel.

Chapter 4 - Extreme Blood Sugars

Now we get to the heart of juvenile diabetes –
blood sugars that aren't "in range". The first thing
you must do to maintain your sanity is accept that
you'll *never* have perfect blood sugars. You'll have
week- or month-long runs of blood sugars in the
low 100s, and you'll think everything is going
perfectly – but then you'll get sloppy, or have a
growth spurt, or get sick, and everything will get so
crazy that your average blood sugar will shoot up to
250 – or fall down to about 70. So here's a little
advice on dealing with the more extreme blood
sugars that you're likely to experience.

HOME HIGHS

Having a high blood sugar at home isn't
actually so bad. Obviously, it's not healthy if it
happens frequently and over a long period of time,
but it's going to happen pretty regularly when
you're new to diabetes. The trick is not to panic
just because you see a 300 or more on your meter
screen.

Be sure to check for ketones. Follow your
doctor's instructions if you do have ketones (this
usually involves giving yourself an injection of some
small percentage of your daily insulin total). No
matter what, drink an entire glass of water (good

advice anyway, but particularly relevant in this case). You may get a headache, so plan to take some ibuprofen or another painkiller, rather than just letting it ruin your day.

While your parents may freak out the first time you have a high blood sugar at home, you can remind them that highs are caused by all sorts of things – stress, illness, hormones (i.e., just being a teenager), insulin that's gone bad, and air bubbles in your injection. After you've convinced them, convince yourself. Just because you have highs in the first month or two of diabetes does not mean you will go blind, suffer massive kidney failure, or die young.

A few 300s or even 400s every once in a while will not kill you. On the other hand, if you're having 500s, 600s, or numbers too high for your meter to read, put in a call to your friendly local endocrinologist and find out what is going on. It may be something like a bottle of bad insulin that you've been re-using, or scar tissue in your injection site that prevents you from absorbing insulin properly, or air bubbles in your injections. Whatever it is, you want to fix it. Numbers over 500 are the kind that send you back to the hospital, and that's not something that you want to happen.

LUCKY LOWS

Hah. Not really. Lows are awful. They may knock down your HbA_1C (see Terms I Use for definitions), but the short-term effects are much more unpleasant than getting a single 8.7 HbA_1C reading. Some people will give themselves too much insulin just to achieve a lower HbA_1C, and while I understand the drive for that, it would have to be pretty strong to actually *want* to endure extra lows (and not wise to indulge).

How do you know you're low? People have many different feelings or experiences. For me, all of a sudden, I have a hard time focusing on anything. My limbs seem to weigh a ton, and I might get incredibly shaky. I also get wildly hungry.

The important thing at this point is to get some sugar in your body. Immediately. Make sure your parents understand that at this point, you're *not* capable of rational thought. They should not hold you responsible for anything you do or say when you're low; you'll find that your brain short-circuits and you're no longer capable of controlling what comes out of your mouth.

LOW BLOOD SUGAR DO'S AND DON'TS

DO:

- sit down and have a fast sugar (see Chapter 6 for a list of good fast sugars)
- do something mindless like watch TV or sleep for 15 minutes while you wait for your blood sugar to get back up
- wait a <u>full</u> fifteen minutes and test <u>before</u> having an additional fast sugar

DON'T:

- walk around or stand up, no matter how restless you feel
- start gulping down nuts, cheese, or crackers just because you're hungry
- try to read anything you need to remember, like your history homework
- write anything that needs to be intelligible
- attempt any detail work; you'll only mess it up and get frustrated
- try to do any chores, especially ones that involve dishes (I've probably broken six glasses trying to wash them when I was low)
- try to have an intelligent discussion (or, God forbid, an argument, especially with a sibling)

Obviously, you shouldn't use this as an opportunity to mouth off to your parents – they'll be able to tell the difference between the random babbling of someone who's low and someone who's taking advantage of the circumstances – but it is important that they know when you're not entirely in control.

In my experience, you might start off intending to say one thing, say it, then have another thought and begin rambling about it. Your brain jumps from idea to idea. Your logic becomes like drunk logic – very basic and frequently wrong. It's awful at the time, but if you were to record it and then listen to yourself, it'd be pretty funny. Embarrassing, but funny.

Shortly after you go low, you'll probably get extremely hungry. If you were really low – say, below 40 – you may be tempted to have a second fast sugar. Not technically within the rules, but speaking as someone who's felt a 29, I say go ahead. Try to keep in mind that this will send you higher later on.

The mid-low hunger, though, should not be indulged if you can avoid it. Perhaps three minutes into your fifteen minutes of waiting, you may find yourself headed for the cupboard or the fridge.

Something in your brain tells your body, *If I just had a block of cheddar cheese right now, I'd stop feeling low,* and because a low feels so nasty, your body obeys. Unfortunately, the opposite is true.

Fat and protein slow down your absorption of sugar, and if you eat them while you're low, you'll find yourself feeling low for the next hour or two. I know this for a fact; raw cashews are my great weakness.

It takes some time to get used to testing, the most painful part of diabetes. But the fact is, it's not going away. Your best option is to develop a coping strategy, like using numbing cream or ice before your shots (doesn't work so well on fingers) or listening to music very loudly as you test your blood sugar.

You'll find that you stop feeling pain very soon. After a few weeks, the needles may hurt, but you won't be freaking out about them anymore. You can get used to just about anything. And though it may not always seem like it, there *are* things worse than diabetes.

Chapter 5 – Food

Repeat after me: getting diabetes does not mean I can no longer eat anything good. It simply means I have to think before snarfing down a pile of Junior Mints at the movie theater. It's true that after you're first diagnosed, you will most likely have a very rigid diet – i.e. an exact amount of carbohydrates permitted at breakfast, at lunch, etc. Your doctor (or nutritionist) may tell you to eat certain things, at least when you start out, to make sure that you stick to the right number of carbohydrates.

Once you've had diabetes for a little longer, you'll be able to choose your meals within a food plan designed for you – and that's when those restrictions really start to grind down your spirits. The monotony of your old diet and the restriction of your new diet combine to make you go crazy craving an entire chocolate cake. It's a bit hard to enjoy your bagel and cream cheese when you know that you only get 45 grams of carbohydrates for lunch. So try these alternatives.

GRAINS

Thanks to the low-carb craze, there are hundreds of low-carb pastas, breads, and bagels out there. I admit I don't like them, but when you're stuck on a diet with a limited number of carbohydrates, you may not have any choice. If you're not into "low-carb" pasta or bread, remember that anything whole-grain is usually lower-carb than intensely processed food. Carbohydrate count also varies among different brands, so if you're good at math and have a little extra time to devote, head to the market and spend an hour or so comparing carb counts in different foods.

For example, Sara Lee New York Bagels are around 50g each, but Noah's Bagels are 75g each – a big difference when you're just learning to count carbs. When you're actually trying to make a meal out of grain foods, go heavier on the lower carb parts (like meat, cheese, or peanut butter in sandwiches, large salads with pasta, lots of bacon and eggs with your French toast) and lighter on the grains.

SWEETS

You can always buy low-sugar ice cream, and there's a wide assortment of sugar-free candy. While the taste may seem to lack a certain something (sugar, for instance), you'll find that the adjustment to that taste doesn't take long. Two

BEST "FREE" FOODS TO INTRIGUE YOUR TONGUE

Sugar-free gum. It comes in plenty of flavors, and it's essentially long-lasting candy. That won't spoil your diet. What could be better?

Tic-Tacs and other breath mints. Don't laugh. I'm serious. They come in all the same flavors as gum, frequently more, and you can usually devour an entire pack of those things without consuming more than ten or maybe fifteen grams of carbohydrates. If you need a candy substitute that crunches, breath mints are perfect.

Nuts. If you're weird like me and went through an eating-peanut-butter-straight-from-the-jar phase, you've already got it covered. Cashews, almonds, pecans, walnuts, macadamia nuts, pistachios, Brazil nuts, hazelnuts, and the ever-popular peanut...all excellent alternatives to carbful snacks. Speaking as someone who can eat a box of Cheez-Its while doing homework, I completely understand the compulsion to snack. For me, nuts are the perfect snack.

Cheese. I'm not as wild about cheese as I am about nuts – much more high-maintenance food, what with the refrigeration and all. But it does make another handy snack. String cheese is always a good bet. The only downside of cheese is that most fancy cheeses – i.e. the ones served at nice parties in a wheel with a little knife next to a stack of crackers – taste a lot better *on* the crackers. C'est la vie.

easy ways to cut down on carbs are low-sugar jam for your toast, omelets, or sandwiches and low-sugar syrup for your waffles and pancakes. Or use fruit – especially fresh or frozen, or canned in water (never syrup) – instead of syrup on your pancakes. It'll be strange at first, but after a while, you'll begin to realize that you'd rather keep eating some form of the foods you like than give them up altogether.

COUNTING CARBOHYDRATES

Believe it or not, counting carbohydrates is my least favorite part of having diabetes. For the first few months, you can only eat a specified amount of carbs at certain set times. Even after you get to use a sliding scale and carbohydrate ratios (i.e. 1 unit of insulin per X grams of carbs), you never get back the same level of freedom as you had before you got diabetes. Personally, if given the choice between no longer having to take shots and no longer having to count carbohydrates, I'd get rid of carb-counting in a second.

It's true that we no longer have to deal with the old ideas about no sugar for diabetics. Speaking as an utter sugar fiend, I can say that making sugar *verboten* would suck. That's our advantage over diabetics twenty-five years ago. But no matter how advanced the technology gets, until

44

someone invents an artificial pancreas or figures out how to cure diabetes, we will always be counting something like carbohydrates to help us gauge how much insulin to take.

Some people use carbohydrate "exchanges", where a cup (8 ounces) of milk is one exchange, a juice box is two, etcetera. This works, but it's not terribly accurate. Personally, I prefer to simply count grams of carbohydrates and then work out how much insulin to take. Either way works, though, and it's usually your endocrinologist who tells you which way to do it.

There are all manner of books (see the Resources section) to tell you how many grams of carbohydrates are in various foods; some are approximately the size of a telephone book, while others are pocket guides designed to go with you everywhere. You can even get them in a computer program for your PC, or if you're lucky, a handheld computer. But you'll find that after a little while, you rarely need a pocket guide. You will learn by heart the carbs in your favorite foods at your favorite restaurants. By the time you've had diabetes for a month you will no longer need to look up the grams of carbohydrates in a cup and a half of pasta or 6 ounces of hot chocolate. For the first month, though, you'll probably be checking a lot, which is a good idea.

Speaking from hindsight, I can testify that if you can get into the habit of measuring your food regularly you will be way ahead of many other diabetics, including me. Granted, some people think they are so good at estimating amounts of food – one cup, two cups, four ounces, etcetera – that they don't really think they need to measure their food anymore.

But if you're a teenager looking to prove to your parents that you're responsible, there are few better ways than to measure your food whenever possible. This will also contribute to your ability to tell how much food you're eating, so that when you can't measure your food, you'll have a much better idea of how much there really is on your plate.

NUTRITIONISTS AND DIETICIANS

My parents dragged me to a nutritionist every month for the first year of diabetes in a vain attempt to make me eat healthier foods. As a snotty, rebellious twelve-year-old, I spent most of those meetings mouthing off to the extremely nice and unbelievably patient nutritionist. Remarkably, we didn't make much progress. Things got worse, to the point that when I was fifteen my parents took me to another dietician. Her solution for me was to make me eat more. Needless to say, this didn't work out to well either. Eventually, I wore my parents down to the point that they eased up about food. The result? I wound up anemic.

So what's the moral of the story? Don't let things get that bad. Make an effort from the very beginning to compromise with your parents. No matter how unhealthy your eating habits, it can't be much worse than how I was eating – heavy on the pasta and bread with butter, a couple bites of meat once a week, some nuts every once in a while.

Everyone will have a different 'big issue' with their parents. Mine was food. It's a pretty common one, since all diabetics have to carefully control their food intake, but it's a really important issue. Since you and your parents aren't neutral parties on this matter, try to bring a third party into the problem – a nutritionist, or even your endocrinologist. Unlike your parents, they won't have spent hours fighting with you about what you will and won't eat, so there's no built-up resentment about "If he'd just eat some salad…" and "She won't touch her mother's roast beef!" You and your parents can each present your side of the issue, and you have a neutral person to give you advice.

Food can be a huge issue between you and your parents that causes endless arguments – or it can be a small problem that rears its head only when there's nothing better to talk about. It's really up to you. Try to be flexible about food. If you can be flexible about food, your parents will have to be flexible too.

Chapter 6 – A Learning Experience

You spend almost a quarter of your life between age 6 and age 18 in school. And like it or not, diabetes changes your time in school. Whether you loved or hated P.E., you'll have to make some alterations in your approach to it. Cafeteria lunches? You may just be able to wrangle a doctor's excuse for a better lunch – or you may have to start bringing your own lunch. You thought lows at home were bad? Wait till you go low in the middle of a final. If high school is a highway, high school with diabetes is an unmarked winding gravel road through the mountains.

THE RETURN

Coming back to school isn't easy, that's for sure. I was diagnosed eleven days before school ended, spent four days in the hospital, and only had to attend school for another week before I was free to adjust on my own. But you may have gotten diabetes in September, or January, or April – all of which leave you in school as you adjust to diabetes.

When you first get back, you have a certain amount of leeway. Most teachers, upon learning that you've been in the hospital, will be sympathetic; some of the ones who never knew you in their class of 35 will suddenly take a personal interest in you. Appreciate this fact, but don't exploit it. There is a difference between going to see your teacher for a help session that they might not otherwise have time for and demanding to have all your missing assignments excused.

Be sure to explain to your teachers and friends what diabetes means for you; one of the worst things that can happen is to have a teacher who won't let you leave class to test for ketones or take a fast sugar in class when you go low. In fact, it's incredibly dangerous. See the Mini-Explanations for an idea of what you can say.

MINI-EXPLANATIONS FOR SCHOOL

FRIENDS

No, you don't *have* to tell your friends. Unlike your teachers, they don't need to know in order to keep you safe during school. But there are several definite benefits to letting friends know. First, if they know what to look for, they'll notice if you go low, and can always be persuaded to run and get you sugar, even if it's 3 AM on a school trip and they have to wake up early that morning. Second, they'll know why you go to the doctor so often and won't worry that you're terminally ill. Third, they'll be around to sympathize when things are going badly. Yes, some people are so freaked out by needles/blood/illness that they may avoid you, but – can you guess what I'm about to say? – your real friends will stick with you. So tell them.

"I've been in the hospital for the last week because I have juvenile diabetes. My immune system destroyed my pancreas, and so I can't produce insulin to use sugar. That means I have to take insulin and test my blood sugar before I eat. *Display testing equipment/shots only if friend is not needle/blood-phobic.* I can still eat sugar; I just have to be careful. Sometimes, I may give myself too much insulin, and I'll get shaky or seem disoriented – when that happens, I have to eat something with lots of sugar and no fat or protein. There's no cure for diabetes, but as long as I take all my medicine, it's not life-threatening. It kind of sucks, but I'll survive. Anything else you want to know?"

THE PALS
"I haven't been in school because I got juvenile diabetes. Basically, I have to take insulin and test how much sugar is in my blood because my pancreas doesn't work anymore. Sometimes I'll get

really shaky and I might need you to get me sugar. Yeah, it sucks. So, did I miss anything interesting around here?"

THE JERK WHO SITS NEXT TO YOU IN ALGEBRA

"I've been in the hospital. They finally let me out, but they gave me a ton of drugs I have to take every day. Hey, blood doesn't freak you out, right?" *Test blood sugar and hope that kid isn't some kind of weird vampire-obsessed person with a blood fetish.*

ADULTS

You can give the same explanation to most of the adults at your school – just alter it a little according to who you're talking with.

"I have juvenile diabetes. It's a chronic illness caused by an immune disorder that makes my white blood cells attack and destroy parts of my pancreas. Because of this, I have to give myself insulin injections and test my blood sugar." *(Show them your shots and testing equipment)* "I may have to test my blood sugar at some point during class. I've been trained in how to do this and my parents trust me to do it." *(The unspoken message: DON'T INTERFERE)*

"I'd appreciate if you just kept going with class anytime I test. Sometimes, I may have to give myself an insulin injection. If this happens, I'll leave and inject my insulin in the bathroom so that I won't disrupt class. Other times, I may be hypoglycemic [low blood sugar]. If this happens, I may have difficulty focusing. I'll probably get pale and very shaky, and I'll need to have a fast sugar. I'll eat/drink this." *(Show them your fast sugar)*. "If I don't have a fast sugar, I may need someone to give me this – it's called Glucagon. I may or may not be able to ask for it." *(Show them the Glucagon and demonstrate, without actually following through, how it works)*. Even after my blood glucose is normal, I will probably be kind of sluggish for about 45 minutes. Do you have any questions?"

PROBLEMS WITH 'FRIENDS'

Most of your friends, after a week of feeling awful that you've gotten diabetes, will move on. Some will forget about it; others will relegate it to a place in the back of their brain along with the rest of the things that they're vaguely aware of but don't really think about. Those who can't stand blood or needles will do their very best to forget it, but will probably remember better than your other friends.

Unfortunately, every once in a while, you do find someone who just can't handle it. The A-plus, have-self-confidence way of thinking tells you that anyone who doesn't like you for yourself isn't worth being friends with. Yeah, sure, true, but that doesn't mean you can't work on fixing a friendship that you really want to keep up. If your friend can't deal with blood, *don't test your blood sugar right in front of them*. Don't give yourself shots in the middle of Starbucks.

However much fun it may be to freak out the guy you hate from English class by sticking a needle into yourself, pretending that you're shooting up in the middle of a restaurant probably won't help with a friend who goes queasy at the sight of needles (it is good for having a laugh with your friends whenever you're feeling immature, though. The other patrons always have hilarious reactions). The best strategy is to feel people out beforehand. Let them know you have diabetes and see how they react before you start driving sharp things into your own flesh.

THE LOWER SIDE OF SCHOOL

Picture this: You're in the middle of taking a major English test. You start feeling shaky, but you're not sure whether it's a low blood sugar or just nerves. To be safe, you test...and you're 29. Sound bad? It happened to me during my freshman year.

School is among the worst places to have a low blood sugar, and probably the place where you'll go low the most often. What with the stress, the fact that you get the effects of both breakfast and lunch insulin, P.E., and everything else, lows are pretty much guaranteed. So how do you deal with them?

First of all, pick out a fast sugar and make sure you have it with you at all times. You've heard this before, but bear with me. See "The Fast and the Fattening" for some different fast sugar options.

Next, make sure you've got a safe place to keep it, and bring at least enough for six doses – nothing's worse than going low and realizing you've just used your last fast sugar. As backup, keep two one-dollar bills with you at all times (stuck inside your shoe is always a good option) for vending machines. And if you insist upon having the money in your pocket because you think it looks weird to pull money out of your shoes, try to remember to take the bills out before you wash your clothes. (Washing machines are not kind to wandering paper money.)

THE FAST AND THE FATTENING: QUICK SUGAR

Juice: Kool-Aid, Snapple, Capri Sun...There are plenty of brands to choose from, along with good old apple, grape, and orange juice. Liquid sugar works the fastest, since you can absorb it into your bloodstream more quickly, but there are certain downsides. If, like me, you have an absurdly heavy backpack which you constantly throw around, I guarantee that you'll smash a container of juice (bottle or juice box, it doesn't matter) at least twice in your school life. This is one of the more unpleasant experiences, since it ruins homework and books and requires you to wash your backpack.

Soda: Carbonation becomes an issue when you have to drink fast and are already prone to choking, but soda is otherwise one of the best 'fast sugars'. It's fat-free and hyper-sweetened – a perfect combination for combating hypoglycemia. If worst comes to worst, you can always drink some flat soda. Disgusting, but it'll spike your blood sugar.

Glucose tabs: In my opinion, a nasty trick played on diabetics – they look and smell like candy, but have the taste of chalk. With a sour aftertaste and a tendency to powder in the container, glucose tabs rank low on my scale of sugars, but you might love them – it's worth a try.

Candy: My personal favorite, mostly because I don't get many other opportunities to eat it. Just make sure there's no fat, since lipids slow down glucose absorption. Some generic safe bets: anything gummy (bears, worms, fish, small television characters), jelly beans, any fruit-based candy.

WARNING! Chocolate is **not** a fast sugar. It has tons of fat, which makes it delicious...and slow to boost your blood glucose. Avoid anything with chocolate when trying to bring up your blood glucose fast. And remember, many high-carb foods (bagels, chips, doughnuts, to name my favorites) are packed with fat and will actually slow down your 'fast' sugar.

Or, tape four quarters to the inside bottoms of your shoes (weird if done to open-toed shoes). It'll feel a bit funny, but then, so does going into hypoglycemic convulsions. Plus there will be less risk of a machine rejecting your money.

Show each of your teachers your fast sugar and explain that at some time during their class, you may have to eat/drink this or something like it because your blood sugar will be low (ideally, they will already know something about diabetes – if not, give them the Teacher's Explanation from earlier in this chapter). Make sure that in each of your classes, there's someone who knows enough about diabetes to help you if you start having serious

trouble. This is another good reason to tell your
friends.

IF EVERYTHING GOES WRONG

Try to keep calm – not an easy task, but it's
important. If you have an insulin pump,
disconnect immediately. If you don't have the
motor control to undo your pump, you're perfectly
welcome to get your set out any way you can. Rip it
out if you have to – it's really just an inconvenience
when it comes to being low.

If you have no sugar and no money, tell your
teacher you're having an emergency low blood
sugar. Don't bother with raising your hand – first,
you shouldn't risk waiting for him/her to call on
you, and second, you can always get out of trouble
later by pointing out that you were low and not in
your right mind.

Make sure someone is finding you some
sugar – some teachers will give you their lunch or
ask the class if anyone has food; others will send a
student to the office or faculty lounge for food. Now
isn't the time to be picky – at this point, you should
definitely take a ham sandwich over nothing at all.
Just make sure there are *some* carbohydrates –
salad can't help you.

Once you've set things in motion, stop
thinking about your blood sugar. Concentrate on

regulating your breathing and count your breaths (or ceiling tiles – it doesn't really matter) or read the wall posters. *Do not* allow yourself to stop thinking and lose focus until you have some sugar in your system. If you black out, even for a second, or feel like you're starting to have a seizure, just yell "Glucagon". Make sure someone knows what it is. Loss of consciousness and hypoglycemic seizures are the most dangerous short-term effects that diabetes can have on you, and should not be taken lightly. It is ok to not be polite or worry about what you "should do" when a low is crashing in on you.

If you're alone at school or somewhere else, find a phone. Do not do anything stupid, like try to break into the cafeteria and find food there. Ideally, you should have a cell phone with 911 programmed into speed dial, but any other phone will work, and public telephones are free for 911 calls. If someone who has sugar with them is less than 10 minutes from where you are, call them; otherwise, if you have exhausted all your other options and do not have your Glucagon with you, call an ambulance.

For more on hypoglycemia, especially resulting from alcohol, see Chapter 9, "You Want a Social Life Too?"

"HIGH" SCHOOL

While not as dangerous in the short-term as lows, highs are definitely not good. If you're at school, they can be especially bad – ketones come fast when you have a high blood sugar at school, and that's when highs do start to get dangerous. After a little while, you'll start to develop a sense for how you feel when your blood sugar is high – tired, hot, thirsty, dizzy, obnoxious. Personally, I get tired and thirsty with a nasty headache. If I get into the 400s, I'll start to feel dizzy.

If you've eaten in the last three hours or so, check to make sure that you gave yourself enough insulin to cover the food. If you haven't eaten recently, test your blood sugar. What you do at this point depends on whether you're on a pump, a pen, or shots, but if you're over 300 (or 250, for some people), test for ketones. This is where it becomes very important that your teacher knows you have diabetes and understands what that means – occasionally you have to go test for ketones, even though you're in the middle of a trig test.

If you have ketones, follow the protocol you've worked out with your doctor. It's important to deal with ketones right away – keep a store of syringes and a bottle of fast-acting insulin protected in your backpack, so that even if your pump or pen is broken, you can always get rid of your ketones. Not treating them is the way to wind up back in the hospital.

If you're simply high and have no ketones, drink water anyway. After that, it depends on the severity of the high. A 250 means your insulin from your last meal hasn't been fully absorbed; a 450 means something's wrong that you need to fix. Talk to your doctor about how much insulin you should take when you're high. At some point, after you've had diabetes for a while, it'll be up to you to handle highs at school, but while you still have parents and an endocrinologist who are frequently around to help you, make use of them.

PHYSICAL EDUCATION

Blech. That pretty much summed up how I felt about any kind of exercise at the time I was diagnosed. Yeah, I played soccer half-heartedly on my school team, largely because we hadn't reached the point where it mattered if you were any good, but I seized any opportunity to get out of P.E. I'm not saying that I'm a big exercise fan now, but I can definitely see the benefits. But there are also certain dangers to be aware of.

When you exercise, you use up the insulin in your body much faster, because your cells demand energy and the insulin has to carry the energy into your cells. As a general rule, exercise will make you go low if you're taking shots. If you're on an insulin pump and you remove the pump (which is recommended for many forms of exercise), you're likely to get high blood sugars, because you're not getting insulin in your system as you're exercising. Alternatively, if you leave your pump on while you exercise, you may find yourself going very low since you'll be continually flooding your body with fast-acting insulin, and it won't take long to use up all the sugar in your bloodstream.

Here are some strategies to help

- Have a high-protein, high-fat snack like nuts or a peanut butter sandwich to make sure that your blood sugar stays where it should.
- Test right before exercising and right after. If you're under 100, have some more food – work out what amount is best for you, usually 15-30 grams of carbohydrates – to get your blood sugar up.
- Cut down on the amount of insulin you take a few hours before exercising; talk to your endocrinologist about how much.

- Try to exercise regularly. If not to keep you fit, or the correct weight, make it regular because it's a lot easier to keep your blood sugar under control if your life is relatively predictable and routine. Exercising <u>does</u> lower your actual need for insulin. That means that even if you're ending up at 250 every time you exercise, you're still reducing your overall need for insulin. It's something complicated about how being fit makes the insulin work more efficiently in your body.

Some P.E. teachers are terrific and will be as accommodating as you need them to be. Others will simply refuse to understand about diabetes. If your blood sugar goes low during P.E., you *must* go sit on the sidelines. Don't be tempted to rejoin the game early because you happen to be the team's best dodgeball player; you'll be no good to them if your blood sugar is dropping. In fact, you'll be a liability. Your P.E. teacher may try to guilt you back into the game – or just order you to play. If you are having a low or dangerously high blood sugar, you're totally within your legal rights to ignore him/her. You know what's best for you – no matter what your teacher may say.

Highs are another story. When your blood sugar is over 300, you're technically not supposed to disconnect from your insulin pump, as you would normally do during exercise. Talk to your doctor to figure out how you'll work out highs. Don't let yourself accidentally-on-purpose go high before P.E. just to get out of it; the P.E. teachers will get mad, it's dangerous, and you do have to actually take part in P.E. to get the school credit. You can't just avoid it until you graduate; trust me, I know.

BEST FORMS OF EXERCISE

If you can handle them – and if you're good enough – team sports are a good way to get exercise. Sports like soccer, basketball, football, lacrosse, and track/field (anything with a lot of running) are the most likely to send you low, so you have to be careful. Since baseball is a lot of stop-and-go, you may not be quite as at-risk for lows, but the stress of games combined with some exercise may send you low anyway.

Swimming is a metaphorical slap in the face; you exercise, which makes you absorb insulin faster, and you're in water, which makes you absorb insulin faster. It's very easy to go low when you're swimming, and a pool is one of the worst places to go low, since if you end up unconscious, you may drown before you run out of sugar. Swimming can also impair your ability to tell that you're going low. So, if you swim competitively, test before and after each race to make sure you're not going to go low.

Not all of us are good enough to take part in a competitive sport. Some of us – the less coordinated – have to make do with basic cardiovascular exercise. If you live in a neighborhood with sidewalks and you enjoy having lots of people see you when you're sweaty and tired (or you happen to look good that way), you can go jogging. Personally, I'd rather shoot myself than have to jog every morning; but it's a matter of personal preference.

If you live near a sports club, you can take classes. Learning kickboxing or dance is a more interesting way to get exercise, in my personal opinion. If you're fortunate enough to have exercise equipment at home – a treadmill, a stationary bike – drag it in front of the TV and you can watch movies while you exercise (an excellent incentive).

Like me, you may not enjoy exercise for its own sake. Most Americans are with you. Just remind yourself, the next time you're staring at a

431, that steady exercise can lower your blood sugars.

FIELD TRIPS

Field trips are a welcome break from the monotony of classes, but they can cause trouble if you're not ready for them. If you're going with your class on a hike through a nature park instead of sitting in class for a few hours, you had better be prepared to prevent some lows. If you're going out to lunch with the rest of the class (or with a club, or with a bunch of your friends), you have to make sure you have the necessary insulin to cover it.

When you go on active field trips – i.e. field trips that make you more active during the day than you would usually be – you're likely to go low. If you know about the field trip in advance, talk to your endocrinologist about temporarily adjusting your insulin. The lowered insulin rate should continue through the activity. Make sure you bring a backpack or something similar with at least five fast sugars and something with carbohydrates, fat, and protein, like an energy bar. That's what'll keep you going.

Test at regular intervals – every half-hour, every hour – to make sure that your blood sugar is where it should be, and if it starts dropping significantly (more than your meter's margin of error), correct it. Avoiding a low during that sort of activity is vital, especially if you're out in the middle of nowhere and your only way back to civilization involves lots and lots of walking. Even something like a trip to an art museum can result in a low if you're walking there from school and eating lunch out.

Field trips can, of course, cause vicious highs. If your French class goes out for lunch, that throws a whole new set of variables into the lunch equation (see Chapter 10 on travel for advice on estimating carbohydrates in foreign food). If you're on an insulin pump and you go on an overnight field trip, you might run out of insulin and find yourself without your emergency supplies. That'll send you high for sure.

Your best bet is to keep a store of emergency supplies – insulin, syringes, test strips, meter batteries, lancets, fast sugars, energy bars, alcohol wipes, and any pump supplies – in your locker, so that you can get to it quickly. If you discover that there's a field trip you'd forgotten about, you can run to your locker and get any supplies that you might need. And remember to refill the supplies.

You can usually tell how good you'll be about refilling this emergency supply by how good you are about the car you drive. If you drive conscientiously and refill the gas tank before the indicator even hits empty, you can probably rely on yourself to always keep your locker stocked. If, on the other hand, you're like me, and drive for several days even after the gas indicator hits empty, and have had to call for help because your car actually died on the road...well, you may have to work a little harder to make sure that you don't run out of crucial supplies.

Chapter 7 – Losing Focus

Diabetes burnout. This is also known as 'that time in your life when you're so sick of diabetes that you'd do just about anything to get rid of it'. You start out with diabetes, and you may hate it, but you go along with it for a while. You can handle it. You're conscientious about testing and you never forget to take your insulin. You'd never lie to your parents about anything diabetes-related. And so you go on for a year, maybe two or three.

Then you realize something. You're stuck with diabetes for the rest of your life. And you notice maybe you're not so conscientious anymore. You don't bother to change the lancets in your finger-poker, or run a control test every week on your meter. You throw needles in the trash instead of in a Sharps biohazard container.

You eat without really thinking about how much you've put in your mouth, and you start to snack between meals. Without taking any insulin to cover it. Sometimes you only test three times a day, or even two. You stop bothering to record your numbers. In short, you don't care anymore. It's not loathing; you just can't bring yourself to do it. *That's* diabetes burnout.

People burn out differently. Some tire of trying to control their numbers and never getting the right blood sugar. So they turn to an alternate method. It involves fake blood sugars – either using old blood sugars that produced good numbers, or simply writing down incorrect blood sugar numbers. They then give themselves overdoses of insulin, so that any time they actually do test, it'll be a low number.

HOW DO YOU KNOW IF YOU'RE BURNING OUT?

Here are some signs of diabetes burnout. If you see any of them in yourself, you're probably either verging on burnout or well into it right now.

- Skipping meals to avoid testing
- Skipping testing
- Testing your blood sugar <u>after</u> you eat
- Not recording blood sugar numbers for long periods of time (more than a few days)
- Reusing old needles because you don't feel like changing them
- Leaving sets for your insulin pump in for periods longer than 3 days, and doing that regularly
- Forgetting to take your insulin often
- Conscious avoidance of taking your insulin

- Taking too much insulin just to get good numbers
- Doing anything that you know will result in an altered number and not attempting to prevent it, (eating lots of food at a dance when you aren't wearing your insulin pump, not bothering to bolus, leaving your testing equipment in your locker and testing only after you've eaten lunch...)
- General apathy towards anything diabetes-related
- Creating fake blood sugar numbers
- Lying to your parents about diabetes-related stuff
- Lying to your doctor

Burnout is recognized more and more as something that teenagers with diabetes really suffer from. Most doctors will understand. Your parents will probably feel either guilty or very angry, depending on how far you've taken things. They probably will feel both.

If you're lying to your doctor and/or your parents, *stop now*. You don't necessarily have to tell your parents that you've been lying (although it does mean you don't have to spend the next five years worrying that every time they say "We need to talk", it means they've found out), but whether or not you confess, you should take immediate steps to avoid serious consequences.

It usually works out better to tell them – there's usually a general family purging of negative emotions towards diabetes, and your parents can be guilt tripped into taking over more of your diabetes responsibility. This does depend on your relationship, though; if you routinely lie to them and are routinely punished for it, you won't be punished as severely, but you won't get the benefit of the whole purging thing. At least tell your doctor and explain to him/her what's happened.

SOLVING BURNOUT

The best solution for burnout would be, of course, to take a break from diabetes. Unfortunately, that's currently impossible. Instead, figure out a way to make diabetes less of a burden. That's where the talk with your parents can come in handy. If they're on your side and believe that you need a rest from diabetes, you'll have a much easier time with it. If your parents believe you're just slacking off, though, it's time to change their attitude about burnout. There should always be someone who can help you out. This is why it's important to maintain a good relationship with your parents where diabetes is concerned – see Chapter 8 for more on family issues.

There are some responsibilities that your parents can take over to give you a "vacation" from diabetes, at least temporarily. First off, you can get easily get rid of the job of recording your blood sugar numbers. If your parents are unwilling to take the job, there are a number of software programs with special cables that you can hook up to your meter and use to download the information. It gives you all kinds of data with your numbers, and you can use that to adjust your insulin.

Adjustment of insulin is another responsibility that you can share with your parents. Instead of having to look at your numbers every night and decide if you want to adjust your insulin, your parents can look over your numbers and simply tell you what to change. It's an easier way for you to handle changing your insulin – or not handle it, as the case may be.

If your parents prepare your meals, they can calculate the number of carbohydrates and the necessary insulin dose for you. If you insist on eating something different, or going out, they won't be able to do this, but it's another responsibility that they can lift off your back. Maybe they'll get you a book to help estimate foods quicker.

There are some jobs that you'll never be able to escape. I found there is really no point in going back to taking your injections from someone else; it'll be more of a hassle, and you'll just have to wean yourself off it again. The same goes for testing your own blood sugar. Why give someone else the chance to puncture your skin? Testing your blood sugar is the most basic thing that you have to do for diabetes, and fobbing it off on your parents doesn't sound like a good idea to me...but if it helps you feel less burned out – go for it for a while.

THROW YOURSELF A PITY PARTY

This is the time for a pity party you didn't have earlier when you were feeling strong. Now, when you can plan it; when you're pretty much adjusted to diabetes and feel a little depressed about it, now is the time.

First of all, make sure no one's going to interrupt you. Choose a Saturday or Sunday. Have all your homework done (or know that you'll be able to finish it the next day, and make sure your parents know it too). Do your chores the night before, or early in the morning. If your parents are the understanding sort, you can always explain it to them – or just pick a weekend when they're not around.

Next, do something totally selfish and self-indulgent. Go to the movie theater and see all three of those new movies you've wanted to see. Go to the amusement park and ride the roller coaster until you throw up. Rent a stack of your favorite movies and watch them one after another with carb-free snacks (so you can eat constantly). If you're bookish, get a bunch of novels with zero literary value from the library and lie out in the sun somewhere reading them. The point is to have a day where you pretend diabetes doesn't matter.

CHANGING YOUR DIET

Diet can be one of the biggest causes of burnout. Every day you have to calculate what you're eating, how it'll affect your blood sugar, and on and on until your head spins with numbers and facts and you'd be happy to just take a pill once a day that would give you all the nutrients you need so that you'd never have to eat again. Unfortunately, it doesn't work quite that way.

There are many ways to deal with this problem; here are a couple of mine. You can figure out the total carbohydrate count for a few meals that you enjoy, and eat those regularly plus extras, so that you don't have to figure out total carbohydrates every time you eat. This works if you don't mind eating the same thing every day.

If you already do eat the same foods every day and that's what's causing your burnout, here's a different approach. Try to expand more into the carb-free arena. That means more meat and vegetables and less grains and sugar. You can eat all kinds of things, and you don't have to think about carbohydrates.

DIABETES SUPPORT

There are times when what you really need is to talk with someone else who has diabetes – someone your age or just a little older who understands what you're going through and has real, practical advice that you can use. There are a couple ways to find these people.

Diabetes camps, like the Gales Creek Camp in Oregon (see Resources), are designed for diabetic kids and teenagers. They do all the work of figuring out carbohydrates, recording blood sugar numbers, and adjusting insulin; all you have to do is test and take insulin when they tell you to. And all the kids there have diabetes.

There's nothing like hearing about someone else's string of 600s to make you feel better about the the odd 450 now and then, and nothing like seeing someone's 12.1 A_1C to make you feel better about your 10. Plus, they know what it's like. You can share horror stories and complain about parents together, sympathize about the lack of nutrition facts on the cafeteria lunches at school, and compare finger scars.

You can also get support through diabetes support groups for teenagers – and meet other teenagers with diabetes too. If you Google your state and "diabetes support group", you can probably find one that meets relatively nearby. Oregon has the terrific Children's Diabetes Network. Alternatively, there are a number of support groups on the Internet that have chats, pen pals, advice, and that sort of thing. No face-to-face meetings, but it's a lot more convenient.

Whatever method you choose, support groups can help ease diabetes burnout. Knowing that there are other people out there who have the same problems can make it easier – hence the idea of "support groups" in the first place.

I wish there was an easy way to solve burnout. Unfortunately, it's something you'll probably cycle through over and over again for the rest of your life with diabetes. Sometimes you'll be "the perfect diabetic", always testing and counting and writing in your numbers, and sometimes you'll be the poster child for burnout. Burnout is, in fact, a lot like diabetes: you have good days and you have bad days.

Chapter 8 – Family Problems

In the beginning, there is guilt. Your parents are sure, deep down in their hearts, that somehow they caused you to have diabetes. Maybe they didn't make you wear enough coats in the winter and you caught a cold that somehow gave you strep throat which gave you mumps which gave you diabetes. Maybe they should have bought the seventeen-dollars-per-ounce baby food.

The Expert Opinion: Negotiating Family Conflict

Intensive diabetes management challenges and stresses teens and parents. Frequent and intense family conflict (cycles of nagging, anger, and escalations) consistently predicts whether parents and teens can settle diabetes (and other) problems smoothly.

Certain types of family therapy[1] promote better communication about diabetes; better communication helps family members solve the inevitable problems that come with the diabetes territory. Some of these therapy techniques promote better listening through structured communication skills. Other techniques help teach parents and teens how to negotiate the mine fields of "strongly held beliefs." For example, parents may feel a teen is not ready to sleep over at a school choir outing. The teen believes staying home would be to commit "assisted social suicide."

Other skills encourage concrete problem solving strategies ("a diabetes contract" or "a diabetes agreement") that spell out each person's role within the "diabetes family team." A parent might agree to stop nagging, and the teen would agree to a "weekly meter downloading discussion". As intense conflicts subside parents and teens feel better. Lowered conflict provides a base for parents and teens to work through even tougher problems and then focus on getting back to regular family life.

Deborah Mertlich, LCSW is a licensed clinical social worker who works with diabetes-affected families in the Portland, Oregon area.

[1]For resources on these therapies see the Resources Section or link at www.rewardinghealth.net.

Some of the many important researchers within this arena include Tim Wyscoki, Ph.D., Michael Harris, Ph.D., Barbara Anderson, Ph.D. Lori Laffel, MD, Annette LaGreca, Ph.D.

Wysocki, T [2006]: Effects of Behavioral Family Systems Therapy for Diabetes on Adolescents' Family Relationships, Treatment Adherence, and Metabolic Control

Even if your parents don't blame themselves, they feel awful that you have to go through something like this while they're reasonably healthy. You can expect that for a while, your parents will be eager to do whatever they can to ease the burden of diabetes. You may also wind up with a couple new things that you had mentioned you wanted before you got diabetes – a CD player, a new pair of shoes – these are "guilt presents".

My advice is to not take advantage of your parents here. It's fine to enjoy whatever perks come from diabetes, since so much lousy stuff comes with it too, but your parents already feel bad enough. Don't try to cash in on their guilt.

Unfortunately, as time goes by, your parents will stop being so wonderfully sympathetic. It takes them a while, but your parents move on with their lives. As you get older, they give you more and more responsibilities. They start expecting you to take perfect care of your diabetes. Something that might've earned you a "That's all right, just do better next time" a few years ago suddenly results in "How can you be so irresponsible about this? We're talking about your health!" That's when you start wishing that you hadn't been so stoic in the first place and told them it was ok. Maybe if you'd complained and cried a little more, they'd help you out instead of nagging you and yelling at you.

Some parents will nag you, but they won't get mad at you for messing up because they're trying to be very understanding. This is much preferable to the parents who don't try to be understanding and feel perfectly justified when they get mad at you. Fortunately, diabetes psychologists have invented something to solve this problem: the diabetes simulation.

THE DIABETES SIMULATION

It's what it sounds like – a simulation of diabetes for the average person. They "get to" pretend that they have diabetes for a week or two – and they get to find out what it's like for you, or a reasonable approximation. If your parents don't believe that it exists, talk to your doctor – it's relatively well known.

HOW IT WORKS

It may be enough to have just one parent take part. They should do everything you do. Make sure they test their blood sugar at least four times a day, including whenever they eat. Part of the point of the simulation is to make sure they understand the massive inconvenience. They'll also need to take saline injections (not real insulin! Saline or contact-lens solution) and you'll have to come up with a carbohydrate ratio for your parent to calculate their saline injections.

They should also have to record their blood sugar numbers every evening (you shouldn't look at them, though – it'll only make you jealous and frustrated). They should test their blood sugar before and after exercising. Everything you do, they do – that's the only way that the simulation can be truly effective.

The Expert Opinion: Simulating Diabetes

A "diabetes simulation" for parents with diabetic adolescents probably sounds crazy, right? Why would anyone without diabetes jab lancets or needles into their skin if they didn't have to? In my clinical practice I regularly ask teens [with parents present] this question - "How did it feel to have your parents "simulate" diabetes for 2 weeks?" The teenagers are usually puzzled and respond with "I don't think they did that." Parents too are surprised because no one has usually suggested that they should "simulate diabetes". But the evidence shows it does seem to help.

In 1988 psychology researchers* discovered that when parents simulated diabetes, it radically improved their adolescent's HbA1c (measure of control). Wendy Satin[1] and team confirmed that if parents "simulated diabetes" by testing BG, writing down "results," measuring food intake, treating mock low BG, and even "injecting" saline solution the overall results were remarkable.

Three months after this experiment ended adolescents with "simulating parents" showed a 1.2 percent decrease in HbA1c after 6 weeks of simulation and family therapy. They compared these parents to those receiving family/group treatment or just regular diabetes care. Both of these adolescents' groups showed worsening diabetes care HbAc over a similar period. So it turns out having parents simulate diabetes is not as crazy as you might think.

Michael J. Fulop, Psy.D. is a licensed psychologist specializing in helping people with diabetes.

[1] Satin, W, LaGreca, A, Zigo, M, Skyler, J [1988].
Diabetes in adolescence: effects of a multifamily group intervention and parent simulation of diabetes.
Journal of Pediatric Psychology, 14[2], 259-275

Two weeks is probably an ideal length of time for the simulation. After two weeks, your parents should be so worn out and frustrated from trying to deal with everything that you have to handle that they'll understand your point of view.

It may be hard to pitch the simulation to them in the first place, though – it's a big inconvenience for anyone. Point out that it's really rather hypocritical of them to get mad at you for failing to do things that they aren't even willing to do themselves. Be sure to say it in a nice way, though, because no one likes to be called a hypocrite, especially not by his or her child. If you can't do it, then maybe you could have your doctor or a diabetes educator ask them.

EXTENDED FAMILY "WAR STORIES"

At some point, you'll tell all your relatives what's happened. Chances are that many of them will know someone who had diabetes. The older ones will probably remember friends who died 'from diabetes' (i.e. from the effects of kidney and heart failure etc.). Others may freak out over whatever you eat.

There are two ways to deal with this. If you're feeling a little short-tempered, take something very sweet, eat it obviously, and then pretend to go into convulsions and die while they watch (WARNING: It is unlikely that anyone besides you and your teenage cousins will find this funny, so be prepared for the consequences when your parents yell at you for smarting off to your ninety-year-old great-aunt).

If you're in a particularly patient mood, you can give them the whole explanation about how diabetes care has advanced. Try to come up with this speech in advance – a 45-second "elevator speech" on diabetes.

You know what to cover:
- the basic mechanics of diabetes
- how medical care has advanced
- how what really matters is the number of carbohydrates
- how nowadays, diabetics can eat sugar *and* live without going blind or suffering massive kidney failure

Sometimes, though, you just have to be patient and accept that your elderly relatives may not, at this point, be able to understand diabetes. Accept their gifts of sugar-free cookies with good grace and send them to work with your parents the next day.

USING DIABETES TO GET INDEPENDENCE

It seems a bit counterintuitive – diabetes tends to make your parents more protective, not less. But you can use diabetes to convince your parents that you not only deserve independence but have earned it. There are two ways to do this. First, you can be extremely responsible and hope that your parents notice on their own. That's ideal. If they don't notice, you can point it out.

Second, you can trade for specific privileges – i.e. "If I can go for a month of recording my blood sugar numbers every night, I think that should prove that I'm responsible enough to have my curfew extended half an hour" or "If I can go for a month without forgetting to bolus, I think that should prove that I'm responsible enough to get my driver's license."

Not all parents will respond to these techniques. You'll have to experiment and find what works best with your parents. But usually, proof that you're responsible leads to greater independence. Of course, with this you have to be prepared to accept more diabetes-related duties – so it's a mixed bag.

BEING MORE RESPONSIBLE

I hate the word "responsible". But since so many people seem to love it, I suppose I must use it. In this case, it just means taking care of yourself and your diabetes. Writing yourself reminder notes, making a concerted effort to test, taking your insulin, counting carbohydrates, exercising, and doing all the other fifteen million annoying little things that come with our diabetes.

There are a few keys to appearing more responsible. If you screw up, don't try to deny it. Just admit what you did wrong and say what you'll do to correct it. Your maturity will impress your parents, and even though you messed up, they'll be a lot more willing to trust you. Do and say everything confidently; don't act as if you doubt your own knowledge on the matter, even if you're totally making it up as you go along. It makes you sound smarter.

SIBLINGS

You've lived with them your entire life; they can be sympathetic, useful people who are always willing to band together against your parents...or they can be obnoxious twerps who you wish had never been born. Diabetes doesn't change that. Instead, diabetes tends to highlight the best and worst in your brothers and sisters. A sibling you always hated may turn out to be incredibly sympathetic and caring when you feel awful from a low, while a sibling who you thought was a saint may transform into a jealous, taunting brat.

TRANSFORMATIONS

In general, people continue the way they were – that is, if you get along with someone before diagnosis, you will most likely get along with them after diagnosis. Unfortunately, it doesn't always work out that way. A sibling who was always wonderful (or frequently wonderful, anyway) can get very jealous when your parents start devoting all their attention to you. A side of them appears that you've never seen before – they go out of their way to eat sweets in front of you, they tease you about having diabetes, they start picking fights.

There's not a whole lot you can do about this, but try not to let them bait you. Ask your parents to try to spend more time with the neglected sibling. You're not obligated to feel sorry for them, of course – you're the one who has diabetes – but if you can summon up a little pity, do it. The whole "family dynamic" has just re-centered itself around you, and even though you certainly didn't ask for it, you're going to get a whole lot more attention.

If you're really mad and you can't summon any pity, suggest to your parents that the whole family take part in the diabetes simulation. That's usually enough to make a sibling who thinks diabetes is nothing reconsider their opinion. Especially when they have to take shots.

THE SIBLING DIABETES SIMULATION

No matter how wonderful your brother or sister is, it's unlikely that they'll want to participate in the diabetes simulation. After all, they narrowly avoided being the one to get diabetes; why should they have to feel what it's like? They feel no responsibility for having caused your diabetes, unlike your parents. And they're probably not masochistic enough to want to give themselves shots every day. Trying to force them into the simulation isn't really a good idea – they'll resent you even more.

INCREASED RISKS

Because diabetes is partly genetic, your diagnosis means your siblings' risk for getting diabetes is higher. Sometimes they do develop diabetes within a few years of your diagnosis, but most of the time, they'll stay perfectly healthy. If they do develop diabetes, your whole family will probably need to go see a psychologist; the issues involved are way too big for me to try to cover.

SIBLING BENEFITS

Diabetes can also bring out the nice side in a sibling who was mean to you on a regular basis. They'll run to get you sugar if you're low, wake you up at three in the morning to test your blood sugar if you have to, defend you from other kids who might try to tease you, and tell your parents to back off when they start to nag too much.

Of course, many siblings will go through both transformations at the same time. They'll tease you about diabetes half the time and defend you the other half. They'll eat sugar in front of you and then fetch you a fast sugar when you go low. It's the whole people-aren't-one-dimensional problem. My idea about the best way to deal with it is to try to understand. Be patient. Remember the good times when they start to be bad, and remind yourself that it must be hard for everyone else, too.

OVERPROTECTIVE PARENTS

It's a natural parental response when a child gets sick: overprotectiveness. Something bad happens that they can't prevent, and they're determined to keep all other bad things away from their poor baby. They suddenly want to know all about every single one of your friends, and where you are every minute of the day, and what you're planning to do and where you're planning to go. They can't leave you alone, because they're too worried that something else might happen to you and this time it would really be their fault. If nothing happens to you, they don't relax – they assume it's because they've been so protective, and so they should stay that way. It's a vicious cycle.

The best remedy for parental overprotection is to reason with them. Make compromises and agreements about reasonable expectations for them to have. You can't make them back off entirely, but most parents will gradually ease up once they see that you're not partying with drug dealers every night.

The bottom line is that diabetes is going to be rough on your entire family, for a long time. Your parents have to deal with the fact that they can't protect you from everything; your siblings have to deal with a sudden loss of attention as well as your hospital stay. I'm not saying that you should spend all your time feeling bad for them – obviously, you're the one whose life has been turned upside down – but try not to blow up at them for every little thing. Remember (I nearly got through the entire chapter without saying it), they do love you.

Chapter 9 – You Want A Social Life, Too?

At some point, you will probably decide that you want to have a social life again. Whether that means dating, driving, going out with friends, or drinking, you'll have to work in your new disease. For the purposes of this chapter, let's assume that some of you out there will drink alcohol before the age of 21. Whether this is accidental (a spiked drink at a party) or with your parents' permission (a sip of your dad's champagne on New Year's Eve), or without it (at the biggest party of the year), it'll probably happen.

THE OPPOSITE SEX

Dating isn't wildly harder than regular life, but there are a few extra issues you have to deal with. There's a difference between a first date and a boyfriend or girlfriend, of course – you don't have nearly the same obligation to be honest with someone that you're on a first date with.

On a first date, you don't *have* to explain about diabetes. If you do something like go to a movie, it won't even come up. But if you're actually remotely interested in the person, you might as well mention it – it's hardly an STD or something repulsive that would harm the chances of a relationship, and it saves you the "*gasp* – why didn't you *tell* me?" reaction that always seems to happen on TV whenever someone neglects to mention an important part of their life. If you do something like get ice cream or go out to lunch/dinner/coffee, you can casually ask, "Does blood bother you?" Or you can say, "Oh yeah, I have diabetes. What were you thinking of ordering?"

Depending on the potential-significant-other's response, either test your blood sugar or explain that you have diabetes and you have to go test your blood sugar. Diabetes also makes a relatively decent conversation piece because most people have known someone with diabetes. If you share the same politics, it can lead you into an interesting political discussion about stem-cell research with the person, making you sound intelligent (always a plus).

Some people – usually the ones whose spinster great-aunt Gretel died of diabetes back in the Depression – will be a little freaked out. This doesn't usually bode well for the relationship; if they're so upset by something that's a major part of your life, your relationship is sort of doomed. But if you're just looking for a summer fling and the person doesn't like needles, you might as well go for it and just avoid mentioning diabetes/testing in front of him/her. On the very first date, you can avoid doing things that flaunt your diabetes.

RELATIONSHIPS WITH A CAPITAL R

A serious relationship – i.e. someone you've been seeing for more than two months and really, really like – is different. Your boyfriend or girlfriend should know enough about diabetes that if you're out on a date or at a party, you can rely on them to make sure nothing happens if you collapse or go really high. In a best-case scenario, your boyfriend/girlfriend will want to help with diabetes. This can backfire, of course – you don't want your girlfriend to start nagging you about testing, or hear your boyfriend bug you about whether or not you've taken your insulin – but ideally, they'll act more like backup.

By the time you get to this stage, your boyfriend or girlfriend will probably have picked up enough information about diabetes simply from watching you, but you can always come right out and say, "Can I rely on you if my blood sugar goes low?" This usually elicits the "Sure – what do you need me to do?" response.

That's your chance to decide how much you want someone else to be involved. And remember, they're not your parents – you can ask for help, but don't get too demanding. It's still your disease, and you still have to deal with it.

THE PROM AND OTHER SCHOOL EVENTS

Girls have it a little harder than boys when it comes to school dances, I think. Boys have pockets in which to put an insulin pump (or a belt to clip it to), while girls have to take off both their pump and the set to which it attaches in order to avoid ripping their dresses and having those odd square bumps that show through their dresses.

But hey, everyone has it equally hard when it comes to food and lows at dances. The snack table is placed like that specifically to ensure that people will drift over and eat...and eat...and eat all night. If you're not wearing an insulin pump (i.e., you are a girl or do not use a pump), the constant eating that the snack table encourages will send your blood sugar very high. Even if you do wear an insulin pump and can bolus for everything that you eat, you'll find it extremely difficult to bolus accurately. There are no packages for the foods you're eating, and you're eating it constantly throughout the night.

It is important to try to have specific times that you visit the snack table – maybe once every hour. Bring syringes and a bottle of insulin (or your pump or pen) and give yourself insulin each time you eat something, being sure to bolus on the low side. Before you go to the dance, figure out how many carbs the average potato chip has, and try to count how many chips/cookies/brownies you eat. I know it's not easy, but it is better than going low at the dance.

DANCE LOWS

Going low *is* a big problem at dances. You can mistake the shakiness of lows for simple excitement, and vice versa, and if you're having a good time, you never want to sit down and stop dancing just to test your blood sugar. It's especially hard to sit out if you do happen to go low; it's the P.E. class syndrome all over again, only this time you really, really want to go back in and join the crazy mass of high school students.

The best way to avoid going low? Eat a meal with fat and protein beforehand, and bolus a little low for it. You really don't want to go low – especially if you're going to be driving home.

DANCE HIGHS

The fact is, a single number in the 400s after a big school event isn't nearly as serious as a really bad low that sends you to the emergency room. Granted, your parents may freak out a little when you come home, but try to explain to them that in the short-term, a low is much worse than a high,

and do they really want you running around
without them with your judgment impaired?

PARTIES IN GENERAL

Parties combine the difficulties of free junk
food, the availability of free alcohol, and lousy
driving. Granted, they can be fun, but you have to
know how to handle them. **The key to parties?**
Bring along a friend who is a good driver and
doesn't like to drink. That way, you always have
someone who's sober, able to drive you home, and
conscious of your diabetes. Every once in a while,
you need someone there to remind you that you
really shouldn't have a[nother] drink or keep eating,
and don't you need to go test your blood sugar and
bolus for that candy corn you just ate?

Groups of friends are also good, but make
sure you've chosen responsible people. Otherwise,
you run the risk of everyone saying that the other
person was supposed to stay sober, and you wind
up as the only one capable of driving the car home
– or they all go off with other people.

Make sure you keep your diabetes stuff with
you all the time. You *will* regret it if you have to
drink a suspicious cup of punch because you went
low and didn't have a fast sugar. Plus, if you meet
up with someone and want to leave, it's a drag to

have to go back to the car and get all your diabetes stuff.

It's kind of irritating to carry diabetes stuff with you, but I've found that the following works well: If you're a girl, carry a purse with your meter, finger poker, test strips, insulin, a few syringes, cell phone, and some candy in case of lows. This stuff will usually all fit in a small purse. If you're a guy, put the same things in your pants/jacket pockets.

ALCOHOLIC BEVERAGES

I could be cagey and impractical and pretend that you will never, ever drink any alcohol. I could simply say, "Don't drink", and while that would probably be the healthiest thing you could do when it comes to diabetes, it's hardly realistic. So I'll operate under the assumption that at some point in your life – most likely before you turn 21, you bad child – you will take a drink.

HOW IT WORKS

The problem with alcohol – and the reason it can be so dangerous – is that it will make you go high and then low. Because alcohol is full of sugar, your blood sugar shoots up; then it plummets. If you bolus, you'll send yourself even lower – and because alcohol messes with your liver, it'll impair the 'emergency glucose' that's stored in your liver. If you start dropping, you can become unconscious in a matter of minutes, and you can die. Sorry, but it's the truth.

If possible, you should already know how alcohol affects you when you start going to parties at which there's lots of alcohol. There are two keys to being able to drink alcohol when you have diabetes. First, never drink alone. You must have someone with you who knows how to use your Glucagon and will be sober enough to see that something's wrong with you. Second, never get drunk. Ever. Know your alcohol tolerance and don't drink past it (generally, a good plan, but especially important when you have diabetes).

Waking up to embarrassing photos and a bad hangover are the least of your worries – go low when you're drunk, and you won't be waking up at all. That means that drinking contests, barhopping, and the other, more pleasant form of shots are all off-limits. For me, my rule is: don't do anything that will result in a loss of complete control.

Follow the general rules for drinking; eat bread with lots of butter or cheese beforehand, so that you're not drinking on an empty stomach. If you don't actually enjoy alcohol and it's a social thing, you can easily avoid it – mix your own drink and leave out the alcohol (harder with some drinks than others), or tell people upfront that diabetes means you can't drink alcohol. People who aren't already drunk will usually respect that and stop bugging you about it.

If you do happen to enjoy certain drinks, make them weaker (mixed drinks) or drink less, and more slowly. Or you can start a drink but not finish it. Leave it on the counter and don't come back for it at all. After all, the only reason to drink something fast is to get drunk (or, in the case of a shot of vodka that's on fire, to avoid burning your lips).

Very important: talk to your parents and figure out what their attitude is towards alcohol. I have a friend whose father taught her to drink at sixteen because he didn't want her first drink to be at a party with frat boys, and I have friends who will be disowned if they even think about drinking before they're 30. Your parents may be willing to let you drink every once in a while at home simply so they know that you won't be binge drinking for fun. It's the whole European theory about alcohol; if you're allowed to drink it, there's no fun in drinking it to rebel.

This plan can backfire, of course; your parents may simply bar you from going to any parties at all, which sucks. You have to walk a very fine line when asking your parents to let you drink. Try to focus on, "Don't you want my first drinking experience to be here at home where you can keep an eye on me? It'd be much safer that way, don't you think?"

Of course, you also have to watch out for things like alcohol poisoning and drunk drivers. If you're making your own drinks, you'll be a lot safer, and you can regulate how much you drink so you won't get alcohol poisoning. No guarantees on the drunk drivers.

DRIVING WHEN YOU HAVE DIABETES

It's simpler to avoid the whole issue and not bother with a driver's license, especially if you live in a city with good public transportation. But speaking as someone who loves driving and happens to live far enough from the city that I'd never get anywhere if I couldn't drive, I know lots of people are desperate for a driver's license. Unfortunately, diabetes does figure into it.

In many states, you can't get a learner's permit if your ability to drive has been "impaired" within a certain period of time. There's a lot of room for interpretation here; usually, it means if you've had serious side effects, like hypoglycemic seizures, you have to wait a certain amount of time before you can get a license. If this happens, then you will want to ensure that it won't happen again. You may need a note or signature from your endocrinologist saying that you're safe to drive.

Diabetes isn't so much of an issue while you've still got your learner's permit, because you'll always be driving with an adult. It's really when you get your own license and start driving on your own that you have to worry.

The safest way to drive with diabetes is to test your blood sugar each time before you leave. This is a really big pain to deal with, and my less-kosher-but more-efficient method is to test if you haven't tested within an hour. Of course, you can go low in way less time than that, but you have to draw the line somewhere.

I've found that it works best to have two sets of testing equipment (your doctor will usually give you at least one free, and you should always have a backup meter anyway), one that you carry with you and one that you keep in your car. You should also have at least four fast sugars, some energy bars (the kind with plenty of protein, like Power Bars), and some other snacks. Keep these out of sight; they have a way of disappearing if your friends get their hands on them.

Don't believe me? Try this easy test. Leave four or five really hungry teenagers in a car with candy and snacks. Return in an hour. Invariably, the food will have vanished. It's a good idea to put a note on your emergency stash that clearly states that *no one* is to touch it without your permission.

If you're low, <u>do</u> <u>not</u> drive. It doesn't matter what the circumstances (unless, perhaps, you're being pursued by an army of flesh-eating zombies, in which case almost anything is preferable to just sitting there). Driving with a low blood sugar is dangerous and irresponsible; you're even more incapacitated than you'd be after a couple shots of alcohol. Don't do it.

Have your fast sugar, and once you test and you're back up within the normal range, eat some protein. Once you don't feel shaky, drive. Trust me on this; if you're feeling weak, you're not in shape to be driving, even if your blood sugar is back in range.

If you start to go low while you're driving, pull over *immediately*. You may have to make a judgment call if you're on a curvy road as to whether it's safer to pull over and risk getting hit or continue to drive. Follow the same procedure that you usually would.

By the way, this is a good reason to ask your parents for a cell phone – if you go low on the side of the road, you may need someone to come pick you up, and other drivers will not necessarily stop to loan you a telephone (or you may not want them to stop, depending where you are).

If you're high, consider the severity. A 220 is unlikely to interfere with your driving ability. Some people can drive perfectly at 350; others start to drive as though they're drunk. Do not try driving when you're this high to find out; instead, look at how you feel when you're in the 300s. If you don't really notice it, you're probably safe to drive, but short distances in good conditions. If you get bad headaches, blurry vision, dizzy spells, and all that sort of thing when you're in the mid-300s, you absolutely should not try to drive. Bolus, and then call your parents to explain or try to get a ride with someone else.

If you're over 500, do not drive, no matter how you feel. It *will* affect your driving. Remarkably, when you're high enough, your breath starts to smell like alcohol – meaning that if the police pull you over, you'll be in serious trouble.

This is true for some people even when it comes to less extreme highs. Be careful.

As long as you're careful about driving, you should be fine. Unfortunately, 'careful' is pretty much the one word you have to remember when it comes to diabetes – you always have to be just a little more careful than everyone around you. The idea is to show your parents (and everyone else) that you can be so careful that they don't need to worry about you.

CONCLUSION

Diabetes will not kill your social life. It may put it in the ICU for a month or so while your parents are still too terrified to let you go out anywhere, but eventually you'll be able to head back out and rejoin your friends. Plus, diabetes is a) a decent conversation piece; b) a source of great party tricks ("Hey, who wants to see me stick a syringe through my earlobe?"); and c) excellent for making other people feel sympathetic towards you.

The key is to remember that these people are your *friends*. They *want* you to live. And they're not into seeing you suffer – they just want to have fun. No one's going to withhold your insulin (or sugar) to make you miserable, or purposely come up with fun stuff to do that you can't enjoy.

So go out and keep having your social life. Don't let diabetes run your enjoyment of the world; do crazy fun things and enjoy yourself. Part of living with diabetes is continuing with your old life, and that's what'll keep you sane when bad things happen.

Chapter 10 – Travel Troubles

Once you've had diabetes long enough, your parents will (at some point) be ready to let you travel. Whether it's a Caribbean cruise, a tour through Europe, a weekend at the beach or the mountain, travel has a definite effect on your diabetes.

NEARBY TRAVEL

This is anywhere that is close enough to drive to. Nearby travel isn't as much of a pain because you're close to your endocrinologist, your hospital, and your usual pharmacy. See below for camp travel, even if it's nearby; you're on your own *and* you're away from home, which is doubly dangerous.

When travel involves a long drive (more than 2 hours), watch your blood sugar carefully. You may go high because you're sedentary for a long period of time (this is especially bad on trips that involve six or more hours of driving) or you may go low because you don't snack or just because.

ACTIVE TRAVEL

Some nearby travel – driving somewhere to go skiing, backpacking, hiking, rock climbing, or whatever – involves such a high level of activity that you absolutely must cut down on the amount of insulin you're taking *before* you go. If you're on an insulin pump, you may want to cut your basals to fifty percent; if you take long-acting insulin, you'll cut a portion off that as well as off your fast-acting. You must talk to your endocrinologist before you go, or risk being a hundred feet off the ground clinging to a tiny rock outcropping with one hand just as you realize that you're going low.

If you know it'll be cold where you're going (especially if you're going skiing or snowboarding), you have to figure out what to do with your meter and test strips. You can't just carry them in a backpack when it's 12 degrees outside; they'll stop functioning. Keep them with you, as close to your skin as possible so they don't freeze. The same goes for an insulin pump, if you have one. When it's time to test, rub your hands together and get your blood circulating again. Try to warm up your fingertips. Otherwise, you'll stick yourself but not get any blood.

On the other hand, if you're somewhere very hot – i.e. a desert – you have to make sure that your insulin doesn't spoil. Ideally, you should keep it in a refrigerator, but since you're unlikely to lug a mini-fridge with you, bring something like an insulated lunchbox and a couple cold packs to keep

WOULD YOU LIKE FRIES WITH THAT?

Fast-food drive-throughs. The bane of some people's existence and the purpose of others'. Whether you love them or hate them, they're a fact of life on any road trip, and as such, they have to be dealt with. The ingredient that every traditional fast-food restaurant has in common is, of course, fat. Fat will make the carbohydrates from whatever you eat stick around. This means that the high from soda (which has no fat) is a much shorter and sharper high than the high from a milkshake (which has tons of fat). When you're about to have heavy exercise, eating fat with your carbohydrates is a good thing, since it keeps you from going low; when you're sitting in a car for hours, there's really no benefit. At all. Try to go for foods with at least some nutritional value in addition to the fat.

Before you travel, go to the websites of some of the major fast-food chains like McDonald's and Burger King; most big chains will have the nutritional information for their foods posted on their websites, and you can use these as reference guides if you end up at any chain. Alternatively, try bringing a small cooler and an actual lunch with you (like a bagel and cream cheese or peanut butter sandwich plus a drink) so that you know the exact number of carbohydrates and you get the whole balanced-diet thing.

it from going bad. A lot of testing meters will also stop working in extreme heat – mine had trouble in 100-degree weather in Iowa. You can keep your meter with your insulin, or simply hold it against an air-conditioning unit for a few minutes to cool it down whenever you need to test. Ideally, though, you shouldn't let your meter get that hot in the first place – it's not nice.

CAMP

No matter what kind of camp you go to, it will affect your blood sugars. Usually, it sends them plunging. I'll talk mostly about 'sleepaway' camp, because if you're staying at home you tend to miss out on certain aspects of camp that mess with your blood sugar, like camp food. For the sake of clarity, assume that there are two types of camps: sports camps and all other camps.

Sports camp will probably require you to cut your daily intake of insulin in half. You're out all day, running around, getting tons of healthy exercise, plus there's all that adrenaline shooting through your veins. Then you come back to the camp cafeteria and gulp down whatever slop they're serving for dinner, stay up late, wake up early in the morning, and start it all over again.

People on the insulin pump may find that it's simpler just to switch back to shots or maybe an insulin pen, so that they don't have to keep disconnecting from their pump or worry about losing it when they put it down for an impromptu jog. Obviously, you absolutely have to talk to your doctor if you want to do this, or risk serious consequences like really bad lows or really bad highs. Even other camps – academic camp at a university, art or music camps – might mean an insulin cut.

One of the best parts of camp: living without your parents. The first few times I went away with a group of other kids, we had frequent candy parties and ate everything that we were forbidden to eat at home. Unfortunately, your parents will be able to tell that you're doing this, because no matter how hard you try to make your insulin accurate, you'll get all kinds of insane high numbers if you go crazy every time you leave home.

Remember everything I said about trying not to eat the same exact thing every day? When you're at camp, you can forget it. Try to find a combination of foods for which you know the number of carbs and can get a relatively decent number after eating. Once you have that combination, try to take pieces of it and combine

119

them with other things – the idea being to reduce the amount of crazy food you're eating and replace it with relatively safe food.

Even bigger than the issue of food, though, is the problem of leaving diabetes at home. When you go away to camp (unless you go to a diabetes camp), it's a totally new environment; few, if any people will know you have diabetes. No one is there to remind you about everything. Even if your parents call every night, you're still on your own when it comes to taking your insulin and testing your blood sugar. The temptation is to get a little lax – eat first and test fifteen minutes later, because it takes time to absorb the sugar, take your insulin a while after your meal, not bother with certain meals at all. While it may be nice to forget about the responsibility, you'll spoil everything if you wind up in the hospital with large ketones – so my advice is: don't get lax. Camp life is hectic, but you have to work diabetes into it.

Diabetes can frequently be used to your advantage when you go to camp, though. If you're staying in a dorm, you can ask for a mini-fridge to keep your insulin in, which you can also use to keep drinks and popsicles cold. Definitely a plus. Locate a nearby drugstore or market where you can buy packaged food (with nutritional values shown) to eat so that you know the carbohydrates. There are enough insane factors in camp life already; if you can take away from them by knowing how much insulin to give for your food, you'll do much better. If you're on a meal plan with a set amount of carbohydrates at each meal, it becomes even more important.

FARAWAY TRAVEL

Faraway travel, to different states, different countries, different continents, can cause all kinds of complications. Time zones, medical supplies, nosy security personnel, estimating foreign food carbohydrate counts....the list goes on. Here are some ideas for dealing with them.

TIME ZONES

Changing time zones is most relevant if you're on an insulin pump. If you're taking injections or are on the pen, you do need to worry about stacking your long-acting insulin. Count out the number of hours that's usually in between your long-acting doses, and make sure you keep approximately that amount of time in between the doses. Keep a number of fast sugars on hand while you're going through this process; lows from long-acting insulin are the worst kind because the insulin just keeps working.

If you do use an insulin pump, the main issue is your basals. Unlike people on long-acting insulin, you don't have to worry about severe lows quite as much. All your insulin is fast-acting, so there's no buildup and backlash. You can simply change the time on your pump, and it'll automatically adjust to give you the correct basal rate. Your blood sugars will be messed up for a few days as your body adjusts to the new time, but that's unavoidable.

MEDICAL SUPPLIES

The amount of medical supplies that you need to bring varies widely depending on where and for how long you're traveling. If you're in the United States, especially in a major city, bring what you think you'll need. If you're going to Western Europe, Canada, or major cities in wealthy countries, bring twice what you think you'll need, just for convenience. If you're going to a third-world country, bring three times what you think you'll need. Many countries simply do not have medical supplies available, and if you suddenly find yourself short on insulin, you'll be in very serious trouble.

Always pack most of your medical supplies in your carry-on luggage. You can replace clothes, but if you lose a thousand dollars' worth of medical supplies because your luggage was lost, you will be without your medical supplies as well as significantly poorer.

GETTING THROUGH SECURITY

Security in the United States is usually pretty easy to get through, in terms of medical supplies. Security people are used to seeing Pacemakers and other medical equipment, so just show them your insulin pump and tell them that you have diabetes. If you're worried about your syringes causing you to look like a drug addict, you can ask your doctor for a letter on office stationery explaining your need for this stuff. An insulin pump doesn't usually set off the metal detector, but you can show it anyway. More often, you'll have to take off your shoes.

Once you get into foreign countries, it can get a little harder. Make sure you know how to say, "I have diabetes" in the language of whatever country you're going to – if you're not fluent, it's a good idea to write it down in case you forget.

FOREIGN FOOD

One of the best parts of traveling to other countries is the fact that you're no longer eating

American food. The downside of that, though, is that most other countries do not provide nutritional labeling on food, so you're totally on your own when it comes to figuring out how much insulin to give yourself. Sometimes, you're not going to have any idea; make sure you always carry fast sugars and ketone test strips with you in case you go low or high.

When you're trying to figure out what to bolus, start off with the basis of your meal. Is it meat or non-starchy vegetables? In that case, all you have to worry about is the sauce. Is it pasta? It's going to be 45-75 grams of carbohydrates per cup of pasta. But recognize that you're not likely to be perfectly accurate in your estimates.

Desserts can really mess you up – ice cream is usually the same, even wonderful gelato, but a heavy chocolate cake in France can be way more carbohydrates than one in the United States. It's a matter of practice and, to no small extent, luck. Just do your best.

CRUISE SHIPS

Cruises were designed to tempt diabetics into ketoacidosis. The 24-hour buffets, seven different restaurants, the absolute lack of a need to exercise...all the unhealthy pieces of travel, with only a gym to compensate.

The best way to deal with a cruise ship is to attempt to keep your eating as routine as possible. Three meals a day, perhaps with an afternoon snack if you eat a late dinner. Keep your time at the ice-cream buffet to a minimum, and watch for what foods send you high. Try to make use of the gym, or run laps around the ship's top deck. Watch for lows too, of course, but when you start out on a cruise, you're much more likely to underbolus for your food and go high.

If at all possible, don't go on a cruise while you're still on a fixed meal plan. You'll make yourself miserable, and unless you have serious willpower and autocratic parents, you won't be able to stick with the meal plan. My advice is to wait for a pump, an insulin pen, or flexible injections.

OVERALL

Travel does make your diabetes harder, but it's also one of the most interesting things you can do...and if you figure out how to bolus right, you get to go crazy eating all kinds of amazing food. Just remember to watch your numbers carefully and bring more supplies than you could possibly use.

Chapter 11 – All Those Other Illnesses

Getting sick is never fun – or easy – but it especially complicates things when you have diabetes. What do you do if you're low but anything you swallow comes right back up ten minutes later? What if you give yourself a massive dose of insulin only to throw up what you ate? And forget about trying to exercise. In this chapter, you can read all about the complications that illness presents when combined with diabetes.

When you have poor control – i.e. *bad* blood sugars – your immune system is weakened, so you're a lot more likely to get sick. Ideally, you'd always have good blood sugars so you'd be practically invulnerable to illness, but somehow it doesn't seem to work out that way. That's why you should be first in line for a flu shot when they're available.

COUGHING, SNEEZING AND COLDS

A simple cold won't affect your blood sugar, but some of its side effects will. If you're feeling too stuffy to eat, you may find yourself going low. This means that you're taking too much long-acting insulin or have too high of a basal, depending how you get your insulin. Sick days are good days to do fasting insulin checks, since you already don't feel like eating anything.

On the other hand, if you're taking cold medicine so that you can actually function, you may find your blood sugars running high. A number of cold medicines have ingredients that will send your blood sugar up. It's usually the flavored ones that will cause the most trouble, since they can have sugar in them; if you stick with swallowing gel caps, you'll probably be safe. If you find yourself having weird highs though, ask your endocrinologist if there are any cold medicines or cough syrups you should avoid.

FEVERS

There's not much you can do about a fever except lie around and feel lousy – and unfortunately, fevers are usually harbingers of worse things, like the flu. If you usually exercise a lot, a fever will probably send you high, because you won't be able to exercise. If your natural state is a vegetative one, your blood sugar probably won't change that much (except when you are on a fixed meal plan for your insulin: then your blood sugars will plummet). All you can do is drink a lot of water and take a lot of Tylenol, and don't forget to check regularly for ketones.

THE FLU

The flu will mess with diabetes, badly. You'll be eating very little, at strange times, and if you do manage to eat something, there's no guarantee that you'll keep it down. You can't really take any medicine to get over it, and you're obviously not going to be exercising or anything like that.

If you're on an insulin pump, you may want to knock your basals down (check with your doctor first before you do this) to 90% to keep from going low. The same goes for long-acting insulin. A low when you can't eat is much more serious than a low when you're able to eat. Not only will you be miserable and sick, you'll be unable to do anything to fix it.

To prevent yourself from going low, don't eat when you know you won't be able to keep it down. When you think you won't throw up, go ahead and eat something small. Wait fifteen or twenty minutes to give yourself insulin for the food, so that you know you're not going to throw it up.

When you do go low, as will undoubtedly happen at some point in your life when you have the flu, use something like ginger ale as your fast sugar. Drink slowly, taking small sips – there's no point drinking it only to throw it up again – no matter how awful you feel. You may have to do this for the entire fifteen minutes, since it'll take you a long time to drink fifteen grams' worth of ginger ale. Another good choice is popsicles, unless you have the chills. Have your Glucagon on hand, just in case you can't keep down the ginger ale or popsicles and your blood sugar keeps dropping.

Of course, you'll hardly be exercising when you have the flu, but you'll probably find that your blood sugars will be either terrific or low. If you start getting highs, consider how extreme they are. When you know you'll have a hard time getting back up after a low, you don't always want to bolus aggressively for a measly 200. It may send you into a low that you'll have trouble getting out of.

IN THE LONG TERM

Unfortunately, not all illnesses just go away. Sometimes people with Type 1 diabetes are unfortunate enough to get other diseases, completely unrelated to diabetes – or you may already have another disease. Either way, you have my sympathy – I know what it's like. I was diagnosed with epilepsy about 6 months after getting diabetes.

Your parents will probably feel even worse about it than you do after that first burst of "This is so unfair, don't I have *enough* to deal with?" You're already used to taking medication and all that crap, and you have a high pain threshold from all the needles, so it's just a matter of adding in one more thing.

Your parents, though, will probably blame themselves once again – "Now he has *two* illnesses, we *must* have done something wrong!" My mom is extremely adamant about the fact that I didn't need to get epilepsy along with diabetes, but by now, I'm very blah about it – they're not going away, so there's no point being mad.

This depends a lot on the severity of your second illness. If it's something like mild asthma (which many people grow out of – I did), yeah, it's a pain, but it's pretty easy to handle. If, though, it's something serious like lupus or sickle cell disease, diabetes turns out to be the lesser of two evils. There's not much I can say, except a bunch of platitudes. And I hate them, so I'll skip them.

It's all about survival. Once you know how to deal with the little stuff – colds, fevers – you can work your way up to the big stuff.

Chapter 12 – Transitioning to the Pump

I dearly love my pump. I got an insulin pump about 14 months after being diagnosed – just about the fastest you can get one, since most doctors won't let you apply for one until you've had diabetes for a year, and where I live it takes several months to actually get the thing and be trained on it.

When I started using my pump in August of 2001, I believed several things. First, I was about to have some of the best blood sugars in my entire life-with-diabetes. I would be 100 at every meal, because with my shiny brand-new insulin pump I would have perfect control. I would eat whatever I wanted, whenever I wanted. My HBA_1C would be 6.0, permanently. The pump was, essentially, my cure for diabetes.

Of course, it didn't turn out quite like that. To be honest, I think I had better control on shots. The danger of the pump is the freedom it offers. You don't have to eat on a meal plan anymore; instead, the only requirement is a three-hour space between meals so you don't 'stack' your insulin. It feels as though the pump will function as a dumb version of your pancreas – but the pump comes with its own set of problems as well as blessings.

BOLUSING

Rather than eating a fixed meal plan, with insulin doses already calculated, you have to start calculating *all* your insulin doses. Your doctor gives you a carbohydrate ratio – a certain number of carbohydrates per unit of insulin – to use when you're bolusing, and you work from there.

You can probably already see the dangers inherent in this system. Most pumps now have bolus calculators, but you still must be able to calculate doses in your head – particularly difficult if your carbohydrate ratio isn't nice and simple, like 1:5 or 1:10. If you're in a hurry and screw up a calculation, you'll be low before you know it.

There's also the problem of forgetting to bolus. When you're taking shots, the act of bolusing is very physical – you take the needle and stick it in your skin – and as such, it's difficult to forget. If you do happen to forget, you realize pretty quickly.

But when you're already hooked up to a pump, bolusing is just a matter of pressing a few buttons. Once you've done it enough, it's easy to get distracted just as you're about to bolus, or think that you've already bolused. Granted, if you wonder half an hour later, "Hey, did I bolus?" it's easy enough to check (your pump keeps a record which your needles can never do), but somehow, I've found myself dropping boluses a lot more often since starting on the pump.

FREEDOM

The pump offers you plenty of opportunities to get sloppy. Your bolusing will lose accuracy because you vary the number of carbohydrates you eat, and you may start to forget boluses. Then there's the problem of specified mealtimes. On shots, you eat breakfast, lunch, and dinner, sometimes with a midmorning, afternoon, or bedtime snack. When you're first starting out, you have to do so at the same time every day.

On the pump, though, you don't have to eat the same meals every day. You have to test, of course, but even that gets a little more flexible. Your breakfast and lunch may be three hours apart, or they may be eight hours apart – and that makes a big difference in your blood sugars. Sometimes you might eat nothing at all for lunch – which, irritatingly enough, can send you low *or* high.

OFF THE PUMP

There's an added danger to using a pump – *not* using it. You have to take your pump off for sports and water-related activities (i.e. showers), or to change an insulin cartridge, and sometimes you're in such a hurry that you forget to put it back on. That's when the problems start.

Because you don't take long-acting insulin when you're on an insulin pump, the minute you stop the flow of fast-acting insulin, your blood sugar will start to shoot up. Once, after testing at 150 at breakfast, I proceeded to bolus, take a shower, and left my pump at home. Halfway into second period – about two hours later – I tested and I was almost 500. I had to take an emergency injection and ask my mom to bring me my pump.

THE GOOD STUFF

The fact is, I'd never go back to shots. Ever. The insulin pump *does* give you a kind of freedom that injections just don't provide. No more messing around with "how much of this can I eat?" and "oh, I have to wait until my next mealtime to eat that". Your food restrictions are basically *gone*. Plus, if you still hate needles, the pump means one needle every two or three days, instead of three or four needles every day. Just stick in your set and you're ready to go.

EXPECTATIONS

It's vital to make sure you and your parents have realistic expectations about what the pump can do for you. You, of course, have been reading this book, so you know that the pump doesn't 'fix' diabetes. But your parents, who want nothing more than to make diabetes disappear from your life, may have some not-so-realistic ideas of what the pump can do. Ask your endocrinologist to talk to them. The pump isn't a cure. It's simply a more convenient and efficient way of getting insulin.

Remember too that just as PDAs, laptops, and cell phones malfunction from time to time, so can your pump. I've had three pumps from two different companies in the last four years: my original pump, a replacement after that one broke, and – after the replacement pump was recalled by the company – my current pump came from a different company.

If you've had diabetes for long enough and you're looking for a way to get more freedom and convenience in your life – and you don't mind learning new things, the pump is my idea of the way to go.

Chapter 13 – A Final Word

I'm not going to lie and say that living with diabetes is easy. It's not. There will be days when you'd rather take a hairdryer into the bathtub with you than go through the same routine again. There will be days that you hate diabetes. Diabetes will cause all kinds of problems for you.

But diabetes is not a death sentence. Diabetes comes with good things too. Diabetes will make you grow up. It may be faster than you'd planned – or wanted – but you'll find yourself skipping past the sort of wanton carelessness that adults seem to expect of teenagers. You may be reckless sometimes, but you'll always have those hospital days in your memory that will act as a warning and tell you: remember, you're not really immortal!

And living with diabetes will make you tougher. It's the whole 'that which does not kill you makes you stronger' idea. When bad stuff happens to you in the future, you'll have an idea of how to cope with it. Once you've learned to live and survive with diabetes, it helps you – and that's the whole point of this book.

TERMS I USE

Fasting basal/insulin check: A method of checking the accuracy of your basals, in which you eat nothing and so do not have to bolus for an entire day. If your numbers stay within 30 points of each other, your basals are accurate; if not, you need to adjust your basals.

Glucagon: an extremely fast sugar, injected directly, for when you're unconscious or otherwise unable to take sugar.

HbA1C: also known as a hemoglobin A1C or just A1C. Finds the "average" number that you've been. 6.0 is ideal, but most diabetics with spectacular control will be closer to 7.0. You can find a chart of the numbers and what they correspond to at your doctor's office.

Hypoglycemic: Not enough sugar in your blood ('low').

Hyperglycemic: Too much sugar in your blood ('high').

Ketones: the substances released into your body when you can't use sugar for energy and instead have to break down protein and fat.

Stacking: stacking insulin means giving yourself a corrective dose for a blood sugar number that you've already corrected for. Causes lows.

To bolus: To give yourself a certain amount of insulin over the dosage that keeps your blood sugar in range – i.e. to give yourself extra insulin for a high blood sugar, or because you've just eaten food.

To be high: ha, ha. Very mature of you (yes, I occasionally laugh at that too). To have a high blood glucose (>180)/ be hyperglycemic.

To be in range: Between 80 and 180 mg/dl (sometimes between 70 and 160 mg/dl, though that's usually used for adults).

To be low: have a low blood glucose (<80)/ be hypoglycemic.

ADDITIONAL RESOURCES

Websites to visit:

Children with Diabetes

http://www.childrenwithdiabetes.com

Juvenile Diabetes Research Foundation

http://www.jdrf.org

Good Books:

A Field Guide to Type 1 Diabetes by American Diabetes Association (2002)

Type 1 Diabetes in Children, Adolescents and Young Adults: How to Become an Expert on Your Own Diabetes, Second Edition by Ragnar Hanas (2004)

487 Really Cool Tips for Kids with Diabetes by Bo Loy, Spike Loy (2004)

Getting a Grip on Diabetes: Quick Tips for Kids and Teens by Spike Nasmyth Loy, Bo Nasmyth Loy (2000)

Diabetes Burnout: Preventing It, Surviving It, Finding Inner Peace by William H. Polonsky (1999)

Barbara Kraus' Calories and Carbohydrates: (16th Edition) by Marie Reilly-Pardo (2005)

The Doctor's Pocket Calorie, Fat & Carb Counter by Allan Borushek (2004)

ADA Complete Guide to Carb Counting by Hope S. Warshaw (2004)

Book Order Form

For additional copies of *The Diabetes Game: A Teenager's Guide To Living Well with Diabetes* (Rewarding Health Publishers, 2006; $16.95; ISBN # 0-9778355-0-2), please contact us in one of the following ways*:

Internet orders: www.rewardinghealth.net (this is a secure site)

E-mail orders: orders@rewardingealth.net. Please include all information listed below.

Phone Orders: Call our order line at 503-816-2689.

Fax Orders: Please complete the form below and fax it to 503-297-5744.

Name:_____

Address:_____

City:_____State___Zip:_____

Telephone # _____

E-mail address: _____

Shipping: Please add **$4.05** for the first book (we ship via USPS Priority Mail) and **$2.50** for each additional book.

Payment: __Check   __Credit Card (__VISA __MasterCard)

Exact name on card:_____

Card Number:_____

Your signature:_____

Expiration date_____

Authorized amount:_____

(Cost of book $16.95 plus shipping

*For bulk order discounts please call at 503-816-2689 during business hours, PST.

SURVIVAL CARD #1: LOWS

Keep calm. Test and take fast sugar. If you don't have one, check: locker, faculty lounge, vending machine. If you don't have money, ask someone you know. Or find someone who looks nice, show them your medic alert bracelet, and explain that you're going low. Give them your doctor's phone number. Try a cafe - explain to the barista. If no other option, find a restaurant that charges after serving. Order a soda, drink it, and then call someone to bring you money.

SURVIVAL CARD #2: HIGHS

Test and give yourself the necessary corrective insulin. If you're feeling dizzy or you throw up, drink water. You probably are dehydrated. If you have an insulin pump, make sure there's nothing blocking the flow of insulin. Don't forget to test for ketones.

Doctor's phone number:

Parents' cell numbers:

Your insurance number:

Your own "low" rules:

Doctor's phone number:

Parents' cell numbers:

Your insurance number:

Your own "high" rules

YOUR SURVIVAL CARD #1

_____
_____
_____
_____
_____
_____
_____
_____

YOUR SURVIVAL CARD #2

_____
_____
_____
_____
_____
_____
_____
_____